Rave Reviews for *Taking Time Off*

An intelligent, thoughtful treatment of a too-frequently neglected issue. This book should be helpful to students and parents alike.

> STEPHEN SINGER,
> *College Counselor, The Horace Mann School*

Taking time off was the best decision I ever made!

> TRACY JOHNSTON
> *Wellesley College, Class of '95*

One of the best books written to help students become familiar with how successfully to take time off from school.

> TED SPENCER
> *Director, Office of Undergraduate Admissions*
> *University of Michigan*

A year off either before or during college is not for everyone. However, *Taking Time Off* offers some convincing options for this worthwhile experience. An interesting read!

> CAROL KATZ
> *College Advisor*
> *Stuyvesant High School*

We all start life as butterflies and usually end up in cocoons. On the other hand, we could take the advice of Colin Hall and Ron Lieber and have our mid-life crisis while we are young enough to enjoy it! I can think of no better testimonial to the value of sabbaticals from college than the accounts collected in *Taking Time Off*.

> CORNELIUS BULL
> *President/Founder*
> *Center for Interim Programs*

	DATE DUE		

FARRAR
STRAUS
GIROUX

TAKING TIME OFF

Inspiring Stories of Students

Who Enjoyed

Successful Breaks from College

and How You Can Plan Your Own

COLIN HALL AND RON LIEBER

THE NOONDAY PRESS

Farrar, Straus and Giroux

NEW YORK

Copyright © 1996 by Colin Hall and Ron Lieber
Published simultaneously in Canada by HarperCollins*CanadaLtd*
Printed in the United States of America

Designed by Abby Kagan / King Kong Cody Design

First edition, 1996

Library of Congress Cataloging in Publication Data
Hall, Colin.
Taking time off : inspiring stories of students who enjoyed successful
breaks from college and how you can plan your own / Colin Hall
and Ron Lieber.—1st ed.
p.   cm.
1. Self-culture.   2. College students—Employment.
3. Voluntarism.   4. Sabbatical leave.   I. Lieber, Ron.   II. Title.
LC32.H35   1996   378'.03—dc20   95-53684   CIP

Excerpt from *Rolling Nowhere* by Ted Conover copyright © 1981, 1984 by Ted
Conover, reprinted by permission of Viking Penguin, a division of Penguin Books
USA Inc.

Fourth printing, 1996

To our families

CONTENTS

Preface   3
So Why Take Time Off?   6
Taking Time Off   9

PART ONE
Working in the United States

Carrie Lee Newman   18
worked as a deckhand on
a boat in Alaska

Josh Fine   24
covered the 1992 Presidential campaign for college
radio stations

Barzella Estle   32
worked as a fashion model

Masa Kenney   40
joined the army and fought
in Desert Storm

Tracy Johnston   46
worked for President Clinton's 1992 campaign

Priscilla Vazquez   53
worked as a secretary to
pay for school

Catherine Uldrich   60
left school when her family
failed to pay her tuition

PART TWO
Going Abroad

Working Abroad   69

Kristin Walker   71
worked as an au pair in
Vienna, Austria

Toni Gorog   78
worked as a field research
assistant in the Amazon-
ian rain forest

Studying Abroad   84

Celia Quezada   86
won a Rotary Club scholarship to study in Belgium

Geoff Noer   92
won a Rotary Club scholarship to study in the Faeroe
Islands

Ben Coolik   97
spent a year in Israel
through the Young Judaea
Year Course

Eric Van Dusen   104
studied at a university in
Argentina, returned to the
U.S. by land

PART THREE
Community Service and Volunteer Work

Volunteering in the United States

Cory Mason   118
worked for Habitat for Humanity in Savannah, Georgia

Brendan Robinson   125
volunteered as a City Year corps member in Boston

Akiima Price   134
worked with the Student Conservation Association in Nevada

Giev Kashkooli   139
worked for a legal defense service in Harlem, traveled to Costa Rica

Susan Steele   147
taught disabled people to ski at a Colorado outdoor education center

Laura Castro   154
spent two years in the California Conservation Corps

Kristin Erickson   160
worked for a nursing service in Appalachia and on an organic farm

Volunteering Abroad

Randy Lewis   167
worked on a boat engaged in environmental activism with the Sea Shepherds

Erin Hurme   176
went on a Christian mission to Central America

Blake Kutner   181
worked with Arab and Israeli children in Israel

Kara Nelson   188
taught children at a squatters' camp in Harare, Zimbabwe

PART FOUR
Traveling in the United States

Ted Conover   199
rode freight trains with hoboes and wrote a book about the experience

Miles Gilliom   208
hiked the Appalachian Trail with his dog, Merlin

Hillary Zazove   216
camped in the Rockies with
the National Outdoor
Leadership School

Abbey Marble   221
rode her bike across the United
States

PART FIVE
Getting Back on Track

Danielle Stephens   228
worked a variety of jobs
to pay off a $10,000
credit-card debt

Erik Brisson   235
realized it was a mistake to
have taken time off with-
out a plan

Alexis Levy   240
got married and then
divorced

Elizabeth Hunter   247
learned "Experience is what
you get when you didn't get
what you wanted"

Chad Hammett   253
left school to work after
earning a GPA of 0.0 for
the semester

APPENDIX
Resources   261

Help on the Way:
Acknowledgments   285

A journey of a thousand miles
begins with one step.
—Lao Tsu

TAKING TIME OFF

PREFACE

If you could be doing anything you wanted right now, what would it be?

Would you be hiking the Appalachian Trail from Maine to Georgia? Would you be teaching in Africa? Would you be an aide on a Presidential campaign? Would you be working for a year or two in the real world, earning money and gaining valuable experience? Or would you be in school?

There is no rule requiring that everyone go straight through sixteen years of school. Each year, tens of thousands of students leave school temporarily to work, travel, volunteer, or just do something different. We hope that by the time you have finished reading this book you will see how many incredible things there are to do in the world. College is only one of them.

We discovered the value of taking time off through personal experience. After fourteen years together at the Francis W. Parker School in Chicago, we graduated from high school in 1989. Ron, who went straight to Amherst College and graduated in four years, now wishes he had spent a year traveling. Colin, on the other hand, spent a year working and used the money he earned to take a year-long trip around the world before going to college. It was the best decision he ever made.

When Colin joined Ron at Amherst two years later, a friend came to him for advice. After failing as a pre-med student, Matt needed some time off to regroup. Where, he wondered, could he find the information he needed to plan his time off? Books were available that offered a Yellow Pages-style catalogue of things to do, but he thought they were more confusing and intimidating than helpful. What he really wanted was a book of *people*—living, breathing examples—to prove to him and to his doubting parents that real students had taken time off and thrived as a result. And, most important, he wanted to find out *how* they did it.

We decided to write such a book ourselves. In order to make the book useful to as many students as possible, we collected the stories of a diverse group of people from all over the country. To cast a wide net, we sent an e-mail message over the Internet which was forwarded around the world. We also placed classified ads in college newspapers around the country, asking people to contact us if they knew anyone who had taken time off. We heard from over five hundred people, and dozens more wrote or called and said they wished our book had been around when they were applying to college.

For two years, we traveled across the country to collect the stories that follow. We found students who had taken time off before going to college and others who did so during their college years. We wrote this book with both possibilities in mind, drawing on the range of experiences that people shared with us.

We hope that you will read all these profiles, including those of people who did things that you would never think of doing yourself. Certain themes are common here—parents, money, when to leave, and why. These issues can be complicated, and our interviewees dealt with them in many different ways. You may find useful information in an unexpected place.

We have arranged the profiles by subject into four sections: Working in the United States, Going Abroad, which includes people who worked and studied in foreign countries, Community Service and Volunteer Work, and Traveling in the United States. The final section, Getting Back on Track, describes students who went through a difficult period, either before or during their time off. Throughout the book we offer tips and information on questions such as "How can I receive mail and keep track of my money when I'm traveling through different countries?"

At the end of the book, there is an index of publications and the names, addresses, and telephone numbers of programs and organizations that you might find helpful, including the ones mentioned by the interviewees. You can write to us c/o Farrar, Straus and Giroux, 19 Union Square West, New York, New York 10003, or check out our website at www.takingtimeoff.com. Please let us know what happened when you took time off, how you used our advice, and what you found helpful.

Our profilees accomplished an incredible variety of things. They didn't have any strings to pull or much money to throw around. Instead, through sheer force of will and a hefty dose of creativity and verve, they were able to create amazing opportunities for themselves—many of them completely out of thin air. The point is, you can too.

SO WHY TAKE TIME OFF?

While each person we talked to had his or her own personal reasons for taking time off, we did find some common motivations.

One big incentive is this: you may never have the chance to take time off again. A surprising number of people, both old and young, have told us how much they regretted not taking time off when they had the chance. Too many people find themselves saying "If only . . ." about taking time off. If only I had taken time off, I could have had more time to think about what I really wanted to get out of college. I have a mortgage, kids, tuition payments, and two weeks of vacation each year as I climb the corporate ladder. When am I ever going to have the chance to take that three-month trek in Nepal I've been dreaming about?

Taking time off could also be an asset when you do graduate from college. Students often complain that it is difficult to market themselves to potential employers when all they have to show for themselves is a college transcript, a stint on the student council, and a few mall jobs. Imagine an employer with a stack of a hundred résumés. The first ninety-nine of them come from students who have spent sixteen straight years in school. Then the employer gets to yours. Whose résumé would catch your eye?

Time off may also give you an opportunity to investigate some of your career interests. Even if you decide that the line of work you have explored has nothing to do with how you want to spend the rest of your life, you still have accomplished something very important.

Sometimes the most difficult thing to realize is that different options are available. The real question is, do you want to take charge of your own life or be swept along by everyone else's expectations for you? There's nothing wrong with deciding to go to college; just make sure you're there because **you** want to be.

Attending college when you are not ready or excited to be there can be a tremendous waste. A typical piece of advice for students is "Just go! College is great, and if you don't like it, you can do something else after your first year. But at least give it a chance." Such helpful advice may turn out to be decidedly unhelpful.

If you find yourself approaching college with little motivation or enthusiasm, something may be wrong. Some people described a curious malady that strikes students who are swept straight into college when they are not ready to be there. It's called the High School Hangover. Symptoms include an obsessive fixation with high school yearbooks, triple-digit phone bills, and frequent trips home to see high school friends. Other students experience the "Look, Ma, no hands" syndrome, when, for the first time in their lives, they are let loose with no rules or curfew. Though the possibilities seem limitless, they often involve little more than drinking a lot and sleeping through class. In essence, many students take their first year off while paying full tuition.

In case the idea of taking time off strikes you as something completely outside the norm, you may be surprised to learn that time off is the rule, not the exception, for students in most of the world. We spoke to several foreign students who were astounded by how anxious American students are to go straight to college and get out as fast as they can. In England, almost all students who study at the university level spend a sabbatical year away from the classroom after they finish secondary school.

The sabbatical tradition grew out of the Judeo-Christian observance of the Sabbath on the seventh day of the week. The day when God rested became a day for people to step away from their work and focus on other things. The Sabbath is designed to rejuvenate and replenish—to bring people back to the rest of the week with a whole new perspective. Taking time off from school may do the same thing for you.

TAKING TIME OFF

People often object to the idea of taking time off. For parents, there is a certain prestige in sending their children to college. They don't want to look as if they've raised a slacker. When the neighbors ask where Susie is going to college, telling them that she is at State U. majoring in business looks better than trying to explain why she's dropped out of school. Students interested in taking time off may encounter a variety of doubts, some of which may be quite strange.

"If you take time off, you won't ever go back."
>   (Of course, because you know how easy it is to succeed in the world without a college degree.)

"But what will you do with yourself?"
>   (I think you're smart enough to go to college but too dumb to figure out anything else worthwhile to do.)

"You'll lose all your momentum."
>   (Because life is a race, and the first one with a bachelor's degree wins.)

"What if you get pregnant, are you prepared to raise a child?"
(Everybody knows that college students don't have sex.)

"I once knew someone who dropped out of school, and he
ended up a bum."
(See the profiles.)

The legitimate fear here is that life is complicated and that
everyone will be faced with many difficult choices. Parents
hope that by shipping their children directly off to college and
keeping them there, they will help make some of those choices
for them. That, you may remember, was the idea behind arranged marriages.

Your family may have genuine and strongly held convictions about the value of graduating from college as soon as
possible, getting a job, and establishing yourself as an independent, financially self-sufficient person. These convictions are
entirely reasonable, and they may lead your family to feel that
taking time off is irresponsible. Your challenge is to articulate
exactly what it is that you want to do and why. If you can
show your family that you're not capable of taking full advantage of college at this particular moment, it will go a long way
toward proving that you are not simply being irresponsible.

To show them you're serious about taking time off, take
advantage of every possible resource. Talk to your counselors,
your friends, your friends' parents. Get the word out. Every
person you talk to will have some new information for you.
You may have to argue that paying for a year of college tuition
when you don't really want to be there is itself irresponsible.
Taking a year off may be the *most* responsible thing you can
do.

WHEN TO TAKE TIME OFF

If you are still in high school, you should go through the college application process, choose a school, and then ask that school to defer your admission until the following year. Most colleges will be happy to oblige, and this will be a big relief to your family. It will also take pressure off you, because it is more difficult to apply to college when you are not in school and the resources of your college counselor are not immediately available. If you are in college already when you decide to leave, speak to a dean and make sure that a place will be waiting for you when you return.

Some people will warn you that you will be behind your peers when you come back. If they tell you this before you go to college, don't believe them. One year makes little material difference in the broad scheme of things, and the fact that your best friend from high school may graduate from college twelve months earlier than you will seem less significant as time goes by. If they are telling you that you will be behind your peers while you are **in** college, they may have a point. Taking time off after junior year in college and then returning to find all your friends already graduated can be difficult.

Others may warn you about the difficulty of being so far ahead of your new classmates. You may indeed return with more maturity and focus than some of your peers. But why is this bad? The concern is that you will be so much older that you will not be able to relate to your peers. The opposite may in fact be true. During your time off, you will probably be exposed to a broad range of people and experiences. Such exposure can only strengthen your ability to relate to your peers and the other people in your life.

A final warning will be that taking time off is something you should do **after** college. That may be the case for some people, but we believe that taking time off **before** graduating from college is ideal. That way, all or part of the incredibly dynamic experience of college will still be in your future, not in your past.

MONEY

For many of you, money will be the biggest obstacle when taking time off. How much do you have? How much do you need to achieve your goals? How much do you need to have left over when your time off is finished? There are three possibilities here. Do you need to make money, break even, or can you spend some money from your savings or family along the way? Since one or both of your parents are probably involved in this issue, you should discuss your financial situation with them at the very beginning of your decision-making process. Your financial status may make taking time off more difficult, but do not, *do not* let it be an insurmountable obstacle. Know your limits, and then find the most creative way to work within them.

Each family's financial situation is different. Your family may have been saving for a long time in preparation for that first college tuition bill. They may also have specific plans to get your brothers and sisters through college. If taking a year off means that tuition payments for you and your sibling or siblings will overlap for an extra year, that may be a problem. On the other hand, that may qualify you for financial aid, or more aid than you would otherwise receive. Also, if you are able to fund your own time off, that multi-thousand-dollar lump that's been sitting in your or your parents' savings account can earn interest during your time off.

College financial-aid departments base your aid package on you and your family's ability to pay tuition. If you have spent some of your savings on taking time off, you may be able to negotiate a more generous financial-aid package than you would have before. But your college may also end up asking you to take out a larger loan to make up the difference. If you are on financial aid, speak directly with a dean or an aid officer. Get them to explain all the possible ramifications of your decision to take time off.

Most student loans have a built-in grace period that begins when you leave school. If you take time off, this period may expire, interest will kick in, and you will have to begin making payments. Obviously, it makes sense to plan for this possibility. In some instances, taking a class during your time off (and retaining your status as a student) will postpone the need to begin paying off your loan.

If your only financial need is to break even, there are numerous ways to accomplish this. Some people work for six months to make money and then travel or spend time doing volunteer work. Many opportunities also exist for people who are willing to work for just room and board. You could also try to borrow money interest-free from your parents or another family member. This has obvious advantages; a loan is not so daunting if you can pay it back *after* you have a full-time job.

People who need to save money will probably have to live at home. This issue provokes strong reactions in people. One line of reasoning goes something like this: Whatever you do during your time off, the absolute worst thing would be to live at home. When you live at home, you sink back into the same old behavior patterns that you spent several years of adolescence attempting to grow out of. Your parents doubtless have certain ingrained expectations of who you are, which are based in large part on who you were for so many years. If you are planning to make any positive changes in your life, stay far away from home.

Others believe that living at home is ideal. Some people's parents have always given them the space they needed to be themselves and have encouraged them to be independent. For these people, the benefits of living at home outweigh any loss of freedom that they may feel. Other people get the best of both worlds by finding a friend or relative who will allow them to live in their home rent-free.

REENTRY

Reentering school successfully after taking time off is often challenging. Many people find that they have gone through tremendous changes during their time off, and this can make it difficult for them to relate to their friends and family upon their return. Other people are disappointed to discover that their friends are not as interested in hearing about their time off as they had hoped.

Try to keep things in perspective. Remember that many of your friends may be envious that you had the guts to strike off on your own when they did not. Even those who do try to understand your time off may not be able to grasp all the changes that you have experienced. They may still look at you as though you're the same person you were when you left. The ultimate test of the worth of your time off may well be your ability to integrate the new things that you learned into an environment that probably didn't change much while you were away.

PART ONE

*Working in the
United States*

If getting a job was easy, there wouldn't be millions of people unemployed in the United States. Finding work is particularly difficult for students who may not have many skills or credentials. Be prepared to sell yourself to potential employers. If this is your first job search, check your library or the careers section of a bookstore for titles on résumé writing, interviewing, and internships. Networking is also an important job-hunting skill. Tell everyone you know that you're looking for a job, and ask them if they can put you in touch with anyone who can help you. Once you find something that interests you, be persistent. It's often the most enthusiastic person who ends up getting hired.

CARRIE LEE NEWMAN

Louisville, Kentucky

UNIVERSITY OF WASHINGTON '96

Carrie Lee Newman's progression from landlocked bluegrass girl to Alaskan sea dog began when she was in third grade.

"Remember those pathetic little floppy records that used to come with *National Geographic*? The kind where you had to place a nickel in the middle before you could play it on your record player? Remember the one with the whale songs on it?"

Carrie's third-grade teacher brought that record in and played the whale songs for her class. "I was absolutely enchanted. Studying the songs of humpback whales became a passion. I listened to more *National Geographic* records in my high school library than I ate square pizzas in its cafeteria," she said.

Because there are very few whales in Kentucky, Carrie knew that she would have to move someplace else if she wanted to study them. "It just isn't possible to fulfill dreams of life at sea when you are in Kentucky," she explained.

In 1989, Carrie finished high school in Louisville and enrolled in the honors program at Northern Kentucky University. "I went to NKU with the idea that I would get all my general requirements out of the way, save money, and get out of Dodge as quickly as my fins could paddle me," she said.

Carrie decided to major in biology and started looking into transferring. She hoped to move to a coastal school after her second year at NKU. "Two years turned into three because I didn't have enough money—although heaven knows I was just raking it in as a work-study student," she said.

In January of 1992, Arthur Davidson came to NKU to deliver a lecture. He had written the text for *Circle of Life*, a book which features photographs of the rites of passage practiced by cultures around the world. Carrie had been so excited by a story about the book she had seen in *Life* magazine that she arrived half an hour early for Davidson's lecture.

"I was sitting in the auditorium, and a man came in and struck up a conversation with me. I asked him where he was from and he said, 'Alaska.' I told him I had always dreamed of going to see the humpback whales there—in high school I painted a big humpback whale on my backpack with the word ALASKA in enormous letters below it."

When the man was done talking with Carrie, he got up on stage and began his lecture. Davidson was impressed by Carrie, and he promised to look into finding a way to get her to Alaska. "He called a friend of his who owned a cruise line and asked if they had a job opening for me. At the time, they didn't."

When Carrie moved back home to Louisville for the summer of 1992, she had already made up her mind not to go back to NKU. She was even prepared to accept a job that involved water with more chlorine in it than whales. "I had gotten my lifeguard's certification and was tucking my tail between my legs as I imagined a long summer of whistle twirling at the pool," she said.

Shortly after she arrived home, Carrie called up her college roommate to check in. "She gave me the news that the people from the cruise line had called. Someone on their crew had quit, and the job was mine if I wanted it. When could I be in Anchorage, they wanted to know. I called them immediately and accepted the position. I had just enough money in my bank account for a one-way plane ticket to Alaska."

Carrie sprung the news on her unsuspecting parents the next morning at breakfast. "I told them, 'I'm leaving for Alaska. I got a job on a boat in Prince William Sound.'"

Carrie's parents thought there should have been plenty to keep her busy right there in Louisville. "They were shocked. They practically stood in the driveway to keep me from leaving. They had a difficult time accepting my desire for self-reliance and independence," she said.

The trip from Louisville to Anchorage was a long one, and Carrie was exhausted when she arrived. From Anchorage, she boarded a bus to Whittier, fifty miles east of the city, where she was to meet up with the rest of the crew. "It's gorgeous up there. Pure wilderness. There is simply nothing out there but you and planet Earth."

Carrie worked as a deckhand and stewardess on a tour boat that made daily trips in and around Prince William Sound. When they arrived back in Whittier, Carrie cleaned and re-stocked the boat. "Days were long, sometimes seventeen hours if we did two full tours. Our passengers came from Anchorage every day. We took them out for a day of wildlife watching. Whales, porpoises, otters, Dall's sheep, black bears, bald eagles, you name it," she said.

The boat also traveled amid dozens of glaciers. "The highlight was the active tidewater glaciers. We could get right up next to those and watch them calve. Sometimes an enormous mass of ice would fall off the face of the glaciers into the sea. People would always ask me, 'Don't you get tired of seeing the same thing every day?' I never saw the same thing twice in Alaska," she said.

The job lasted until late September, and the boat headed down to Seattle. "I walked around alone the night we arrived and instantly fell in love with Seattle. It was one of the most striking cities I had ever seen," she said.

The next morning, Carrie boarded the plane home to Louisville. "I had obligations to tie up at home before I could make the move out west. Kentucky was great for about a week, but after that I was just overwhelmed with a feeling of stagnation. I had seen all these things I had waited so long to see. How could I settle for the river when I could have the ocean?"

Carrie got a job at Victoria's Secret and started to pool her earnings with her Alaska money. She had begun to save for what she hoped would be her move to a coastal school. Her parents, on the other hand, wanted her to reenroll at NKU and get her degree.

"I finally told them one day, very calmly, 'What you don't understand is that I am going to leave. I am not asking for your permission, but I would like your blessing.' " With that, Carrie packed up her car in March of 1993 and left Kentucky for good.

"Up in Alaska, someone told me about the program at the University of Washington in Seattle. During my time back in Kentucky, I had researched the school and found the tuition to be reasonable. Plus, I adored Seattle. I would move there, try to get into UW, and work on establishing my residency to get the tuition down," she said.

But not before she went to Alaska for another season. This time, Carrie had gotten a job on a boat that was in a bad state of repair. "I began to assist in the total overhaul of the boat from the water up. It was grueling work, but I actually enjoyed it. I was the only woman in the shipyard. It was quite an experience, going from Victoria's Secret in my stockings and heels to a shipyard in my coveralls, knee pads, and hard hat," she said.

The boat sailed north in May, and Carrie spent her second summer cruising the whale-laden waters of Prince William Sound. At the same time, she applied to the University of Washington for the fall. They rejected her.

Refusing to take no for an answer, Carrie asked two former professors at NKU to write letters of recommendation to the board of admissions. She successfully appealed its decision and was admitted to UW for the winter quarter of 1994.

"I was lucky. By the grace of the gods, nearly every single credit from NKU transferred. I had managed to complete all my general requirements as far as UW was concerned and could focus on my degree work," she said.

Carrie's persistence had won her parents over and they were now supporting her ambitions. Despite their help with tuition costs, however, she still had to work full-time as an office manager to support herself.

"I found I had little in common with other college students who were completely supported by their parents. My job always came first. I had to skip classes for work because they were depending on me for one thing or another," she said.

Carrie plans to graduate from the University of Washington in May of 1996 and then pursue a Ph.D. "They change the name of my field by the minute. Cetology, marine biology, psychology/animal behavior, biological oceanography, you name it. I want to study the humpback populations in the Southern Hemisphere, because those whales are largely undocumented," she said.

She has also logged enough hours at sea to qualify for a license which allows her to operate some boats under certain conditions. After one more summer, she will be eligible for her captain's license, which will give her even more of a passport to the world's oceans.

"That's been the goal all along. To break out from under the burden of my own limitations."

JOSH FINE

Chicago, Illinois
UNIVERSITY OF MICHIGAN '95

The light bulbs started going off in Josh Fine's head as he strolled down Thirty-fourth Street in New York City during the summer of 1992.

Josh was working at the Democratic National Convention. He spent much of his time running errands as a page for the Democratic National Committee, but he also did some reporting for the radio station at the University of Michigan.

"I was walking from DNC headquarters to Madison Square Garden, and I started thinking about all the reporters who were there from all over the world," he recalled. "Issues kept coming up that directly related to college students, but no cohesive group of college reporters was there to interpret them.

"I had been keeping a journal of everything I observed at the convention. My roommate was always asleep, so I would go down to the hotel bar to write. That night I just sat there for hours, spitting out all these ideas."

When he returned home to Chicago a few days later, he

sat his father down for a talk. "I told him that I had this crazy idea—to take time off to build a network of college radio stations to cover the Presidential campaign. I told him that I would need to raise a lot of money, find stations to carry the reports, and a bunch of other things. I knew there was not a lot of time to pull it together.

"My father suggested I talk to some people in the media business about it. He actually never had a problem with the idea of my taking time off, as long as it was to do something moderately productive."

Josh approached a few industry types, and they were excited. "They were clear that it could, that it *needed* to happen, so after that I knew it was at least a possibility," he said.

An executive at NBC in Chicago whom he met through a summer internship was his most helpful advisor. She walked him through the long list of logistical issues he would need to address to set up a one-man network in less than six weeks.

"She was amazing. She knew exactly what it would cost, what I needed to do technically, that I had to target stations in swing states, where the student votes would really matter, so the campaign would take me seriously," he said. "Never in my wildest dreams would I have been able to put all that together in my head."

The technical aspects of building the network were easy enough. Josh found a company that gave him a free voice-mail box, so he could call in every day and record his reports for the client stations to retrieve on their own.

But he soon realized how difficult it was going to be to finance the operation. "At first, we figured I would need $50,000 to finance the project, but we eventually lowered that number dramatically. We quickly found out that there is no money in college radio. We were hoping to get a hundred stations to pay $300 each. Many stations were interested, but few of them could pay. We ended up giving the reports away to several stations," he said.

Josh went to foundations, corporate sponsors, and many individuals for financial support, and was turned away regularly. "It became clear that this was not the way to go," Josh recalled. "As curious as people seemed to be, no one wanted to touch anything that looked at all political."

Eventually, Josh tapped into a nationwide network of voter-education projects. Bit by bit, tiny grant by tiny grant, he collected enough to finance his first few weeks on the road.

Josh knew that he would need to spend about seventy-five percent of his time with Bill Clinton, since Clinton seemed to spend much more time addressing issues that concerned college students than did Bush. His final task was getting a seat on the Clinton campaign plane. "I had to push hard for that, but I was definitely the right reporter at the right time," Josh explained. "They were targeting the youth vote, and I came in with a large number of potential listeners." He told the campaign that he would start around Labor Day.

As his departure date drew near, Josh still did not have enough money to stay on the road through Election Day. "I had about $7,500, nowhere near enough money to finish. I thought maybe I should just say, 'Hey, I gave it my best shot, but it didn't turn out the way that I wanted and life goes on,' " he recalled.

"But my dad said to go—that once I was actually out there making it happen and getting some publicity, it would be easier to raise the money. And if worst came to worst, I would come home at the end of September.

"Shortly before I left to join the campaign, I stayed up talking with a friend almost all night. She told me, 'You could regret not going, but you'll never regret having given it your best shot.' "

So Josh left a few days later with a mental list of the issues that he wanted to cover. "A lot of issues in this campaign had a specific bearing on young people's lives," he said. "Some of them, like the national debt, had gotten a lot of play in the national press. But others, like the environment and the economics of national service, were really almost untouched by the media as a whole."

Josh flew to Portland, Oregon, just as his friends were returning to Ann Arbor. "Their reaction was a mix of 'You're crazy' and 'That's the greatest idea I've ever heard,' " Josh recalled. "I knew I would miss school, but I never really minded taking the semester off. I knew there was just no other way to do it."

When Josh got off the plane, he lugged his bags to the first rally of the day and was greeted by pandemonium. "It was the biggest trip ever," he said. "There were people screaming 'Traveling press, traveling press,' and I remember thinking, 'Oh, they must mean me.'

"They treated us like royalty," Josh said. "I was on these planes and buses with people like Gwen Ifill from *The New York Times* and Mara Liasson from National Public Radio. I was completely starry-eyed."

That first day, Josh traveled to Eugene, Oregon, where he reported on an environmental rally. Later that day, he took his first ride on the press plane to San Francisco.

"They called the press plane the zoo plane, and it was the greatest thing ever," Josh said. "I learned more on that plane with those hundred and fifty reporters than anywhere else. It **was** kind of like a zoo—a giant traveling fraternity—with streamers everywhere and food and beer. God, those are really the best memories I have.

"I had hoped the whole experience would be fun, but I didn't expect it to be. I thought it would be really lonely, out in random cities with reporters who were all older, who would not give a shit about me, sitting in hotel rooms by myself and working really hard."

Instead, Josh was surprised at how quickly people took to him. "I think they were excited by what I was doing and excited to have a young person around," he said. "I was amazed by the friendliness of it all."

Meanwhile, friends at home were seeking additional financial support on his behalf, and Josh said that the other reporters also helped him out. "They've all got these basically unlimited expense accounts, so they were really nice about picking up the tab when we went out or letting me crash in their rooms if there was an extra bed," he said.

Josh found other ways to save as well. He flew commercial flights at times, since traveling on the campaign plane costs more than first-class on an airline. He stayed with friends when he could and managed to stay in Chicago for a few weekends as well.

Though Josh ended up spending about eighty percent of his time with Clinton, he spent enough time with Bush to see how markedly different their campaigns were. "I did a whole story one day on the music they played at their campaign stops. Bush played Presidential-march-type music, and Clinton played Arrested Development. You get the idea," he said.

Josh filed at least one story to his voice-mail box each day, often focusing on a speech the candidate had made. "I tried to focus on a particular speech or appearance and then have a representative from the opposing candidate sound-biting their response. That way, I didn't get any complaints about balance," he said.

Josh said that his best moments professionally came when

he asked questions that the candidates were not expecting. "I was at a press conference where a high-level admiral from the Reagan/Bush years announced his endorsement of Clinton. It was pretty civil," he recalled.

Civil, that is, until the admiral stunned the room into silence by answering Josh's question about Clinton's plan to allow gays in the military. "He said he didn't agree at all, but that he was sure Clinton was open-minded enough to consider all sides of that issue," Josh recalled.

"That was my proudest moment. All these veteran reporters came up to me afterwards and said that that was the best question of the news conference," he said. "That was one of my best stories of the campaign, because it was my voice actually asking the question."

Josh also landed a very brief one-on-one interview with Clinton a few days before the election. Clinton was backstage at the Meadowlands in East Rutherford, New Jersey, when campaign press secretary Dee Dee Myers sent an aide to bring Josh, who had been clamoring for a one-on-one for several weeks, to the holding area where Clinton was waiting to make a speech.

" 'Okay, Josh, now's your chance,' she told me. 'You get one question.' I had about five minutes to decide, to think about the one issue that was on the minds of all young people," he said.

"I finally decided on national service, an idea that got huge applause at every stop, and I think it's safe to say was a total fraud," he said. "Clinton was essentially saying that everyone could pay for college by working for two years, which was not at all what ended up being submitted to Congress."

Josh did not want to push him too hard, however. "That's one of the most disappointing things I learned about the whole process. You have to ask your questions in only a moderately challenging way, because if you don't, you lose access altogether," he said. Clinton told Josh that he thought his promises were fair and his proposals were financially feasible. He eventually proposed a program that would include 70,000 participants by 1997.

As the campaign wound down, Josh made plans to be in Little Rock for the victory celebration. After a few days of covering meetings on the transition, he returned to Chicago to wait for the second semester of school to begin.

"I was absolutely thrilled to go back to school," he said. "It was so nice to be somewhere where my only job was to do my homework, and everyone was my own age again. It was refreshing after spending all my time with thirty- and forty-year-olds for three months."

Though Josh missed the adrenaline surge from the daily reporting grind, his experiences helped him develop a different attitude about school. "I learned that these people in my field, the top people, most of them did go to college, but they can't remember what they took, got poor grades in the classes they can remember, and didn't necessarily go to good schools in the first place," he said. "My new attitude was basically that I would take full advantage of the things that really interested me, and those that didn't, I just wouldn't worry about."

Back in school, Josh put his journalism skills to work by hosting a weekly political talk show known as *By the People*. He also worked as the sports director for the university's radio station. After graduating as a political science major in May of 1995, Josh went to work as a sports writer for Delphi, an online service.

Josh agreed that it might seem intimidating for anyone to try to reproduce what he did in future campaigns. But he insisted that it's not out of reach for most college students with some radio experience. "It was just a question of drive, having the will to stay up until four in the morning faxing things off and making it happen. It took a lot of chutzpah, but it was not a smarts kind of thing. I didn't have any more smarts than anyone else."

BARZELLA ESTLE

Saraland, Alabama

UNIVERSITY OF ALABAMA '95

Barzella Estle's high school class in Saraland, Alabama, a suburb fifteen miles outside of Mobile, graduated 250 kids. After high school, almost half of them got married, half went to community colleges, and a few went directly to four-year colleges. Barzella, however, ended up in the pages of *Seventeen*.

"I had never taken people seriously before when they told me I should model. My best friend in high school, Ava, she was captain of the dance line, and all the guys were always like 'Oooh, Ava, she's so hot.' No one ever gave me a second look.

"It's like a big joke when I go home now. One time, some guys came over, and they said, 'Barzella, why didn't you ever go out in high school.' And my mom says right back to them, 'Well, hell, no one ever asked her.' "

During her senior year in high school, Barzella worked for Gayfers, a local department store. "It was my sister's second husband who finally convinced me to ask them if I could try modeling for them. My boss, who was the public relations director for the store, liked me a lot. She ended up using me for local newspaper ads and then I ended up in the ad in the back-to-school issue of *Seventeen*.

"It boosted my self-confidence a lot. I thought maybe I just had something going for me that no one else had noticed yet."

Barzella was so preoccupied with going to college that she didn't seriously consider the possibility of modeling full-time. "In Alabama, college football is a religion, and I grew up loving the University of Alabama Crimson Tide. I got scholarship offers from smaller schools, but it was either Alabama or bust," she said.

When Barzella arrived in Tuscaloosa, however, she found that there was much more to school than the Saturday game. "It's a very Greek-oriented school. If you're not in a fraternity or a sorority, you're not anything. So I went through rush, but I just wasn't from the right family. None of the good sororities picked me up. No one knew who I was."

Barzella made the best of it and pledged one of the newest sororities on campus. "The money part was ridiculous. They fined you for missing chapter meetings or not wearing your Greek letters on Friday. It costs more to pay house dues and be in a sorority at Alabama than it does to pay tuition. I depledged after two months, and I was an instant nonperson. I felt like such a huge outcast. All the rich girls and pretty girls were here or there, and I just didn't fit in," she said.

To make matters worse, Barzella was also struggling academically. "I had no idea what I was in for. I kept my nose in the books in high school, but the public-school system in Alabama just isn't very good, and I was not prepared at all. I basically just paddled through my classes, and I didn't get above a 2.5 my first three semesters," she said.

Before she even had a chance to transfer, however, she had a lucky break. "After my senior year in high school, *Model* magazine was holding a cover-girl contest, so I sent a few pictures in and didn't think anything of it," she explained.

"Right after my first set of finals in December of my freshman year, I was in the grocery store with my roommates, and they had *Model* in the magazine rack. The cover had a teaser about the cover-girl finalists, and I opened it up and said, 'Oh my God!' My girlfriend, she just started screaming, 'That's you, that's you!' They had never called to tell me.

"I didn't win, but that really sparked my interest. The bug had hit me, and I wanted to see what I could do with it. I found a woman who ran a small modeling agency in Birmingham, and the summer after my freshman year she took me to a national modeling convention. It turned out that a new New York agency that had been profiled in *Model* the same issue that I was in was at the convention. They remembered me and signed me up," she said.

By then, Barzella already had registered to begin her sophomore year, so she agreed to move to New York City at the end of the semester. "I went back to school, and I shouldn't have. I didn't care about anything except getting the hell out of Alabama. I did so horribly that semester, I was so ashamed. I should have filed for academic bankruptcy," she said.

When winter finally arrived, Barzella bought a one-way Amtrak ticket to New York City. "I didn't think twice about what it meant to move to New York. I had my two footlockers and my jam box, and off I went.

"My agency didn't have an apartment for the models, so they had set me up with a room at a Salvation Army all-women boardinghouse. It was real secure, and it was good for my transition. Later on, I ended up moving into an apartment with someone I met through work," she said.

Barzella visited her new agency the day after her arrival, and they already had arranged a number of auditions for her.

Since she didn't have any idea where any of them were, she decided it would be best to learn the city methodically first.

"I studied the map for three days. I studied the subway, the building numbers, and which way the traffic went, so I could look nonchalant, like I knew where I was going," she said.

Even though she had planned to do printwork, she found her way to an audition for a Heineken commercial. "It ended up being my first job. We filmed it at night on the Brooklyn Bridge. It was in January, and it was so cold. It took seven hours," she said.

As if she needed any further evidence that the workday of a New York model isn't all glitz and glamour, the grueling audition process drove it home. "They would examine you from head to toe. Some of them would make you put on a bathing suit and come out and turn around. Others would measure every part of your body and then take Polaroids.

"I hated being on the spot. One day I was out running errands, just in grubby clothes or whatever, and I stopped by my agency to pick up a check. My agent said, 'You know, Barzella, you really need to work on your appearance.' I was always on display."

The scoldings that Barzella received from her agent were a not-so-gentle reminder that she was a bit out of her element, but she tried not to let it bother her. "It was like going to Mars. When I first moved there, no one could understand me because I talked so fast and my accent was so Southern. I made an idiot of myself on many occasions, with the wrong attire, or not having the proper manners, or just blurting out the wrong English," she said.

She took comfort in the fact that she was not the only model in New York to have been plucked out of a small town. "One of my best friends there came from Shinglehouse, Pennsylvania. She's now married to a power broker and living in a fancy apartment on the Upper East Side. Her husband is sending her to cooking school," she added.

"It was kind of nice, actually. The agency sometimes would take all the girls out to dinner, and they would have agency parties. It was kind of like the sorority I never got into at Alabama. I had no problem making friends in New York."

Though the work wasn't steady at first, by the end of the spring it began to pick up. "Eventually, I was working at least once a week. I did *Glamour*, *Mademoiselle*, and a shoot for *Woman's World*, where they made me look like I was about thirty. Then there was this one where I was in a wedding gown. I told my mom to buy twenty copies of that one because it was the last time she would ever see me in a wedding dress!"

The pay was generally excellent, but Barzella soon discovered that there was an inverse relationship between the size of her check and the prestige of the job. "The bridal thing paid $1,500 for four hours, and when you would work in a showroom trying on new clothes for reps from department stores, you'd make about $150 an hour. But *Glamour* paid like $150 a day, because girls would kill to do that," she said.

Sometimes, however, even the best payday wasn't worth what she had to put up with. "There were a lot of slimeballs trying to get a little too cozy after the shoot. I would finally get comfortable with a photographer, but when they make a pass at you, it just ruins the chemistry," she said.

Barzella became friends with the owner of a restaurant on the Upper East Side of Manhattan, and she decided to take a job as a hostess to have more of a regular cash flow. The restaurant, it turned out, was a hangout for all sorts of interesting characters.

"I got to know one of New York's crime families pretty well. One of the big guys in the family kind of liked me, and he invited me to their Christmas party. They had covered up the windows of the restaurant with fake snow so that the federal agents outside could not see who was inside," she said.

"I also ran the music at night at the restaurant. Two guys from Miami were there one night, and they were starting a party called Disco Inferno at the Roxy, this great club. They asked me if I wanted to learn how to work a real turntable, and the next thing I knew I was the DJ at their party.

"So, by then, I was studying at the Actors Institute on Monday nights, going out on casting calls and modeling during the day, working at the restaurant on other nights, and working at the Roxy till 5 a.m. on Fridays. Then on Saturday I'd watch college football. I wouldn't even answer the phone. I had to see how Alabama was doing," she said.

Alabama, it turned out, was equally concerned with how Barzella was doing. Her mother and her stepfather, who had never been to New York, drove up to see her. "I ended up getting booked the days they were here. I left them maps and directions and everything, but I don't think they went outside the apartment once without me. They were petrified.

"I had an uncle come to visit me, and he said, 'Now, you're not doing drugs or anything, are you, Barzella?' All my family, they prayed for me at night. I think they thought I had gone off on the wrong track. They couldn't really comprehend the life I was leading."

It seemed that life couldn't get any crazier, until Barzella began her affair with a prominent former NFL football player. "A sportscaster who hung out at the restaurant introduced me to him, and we ended up being involved for two years. He was still kind of married when we started dating, but they had been having problems for a while." Try explaining that to your parents back home in Alabama.

After almost two years, the pace began to wear on Barzella, and she began to think about going back to school. "I investigated New York University, but my grades were too low to get in there or anyplace else really. Alabama was so cheap, and my parents wanted me to come back because they knew I was going to lose my residency status. So I decided to go back," she said.

Not before she talked it over with a few of her trusted advisors, however. "O. J. Simpson used to hang out at the restaurant a lot. When I told him I was going to go to school again, he told me I was going backwards and making a huge mistake. He kept saying, 'You don't go from Alabama to New York back to Alabama! You go from Alabama to New York to L.A.' "

After two years in New York City, returning to Tuscaloosa was a letdown. "Being stuck there with all these fratdaddies and sorority girls—I guess I did have some readjustment problems," she said.

Barzella coped by throwing herself into her academic work. "Being in New York, I saw a lot of B.S. It finally hit me that I wasn't really all that aware of what was going on around me. I was so caught up in modeling and the fast-paced jetsetting that academically I was, well, not dumb, but just behind," she said.

She also discovered some hidden talents. "Originally, I was going to major in public relations. That's what my boss had done at Gayfers, and I liked her job. So I was taking mass communications, and in the lab we had a lot of writing to do. I found out that I had a knack for writing in the journalistic style, and all of a sudden I was making A's. I started volunteering for the school newspaper, and eventually I got paid jobs working for the university. Now maybe I can go back into the fashion-magazine business on the other side," she explained.

Barzella encourages anyone with raw talent—whatever the field—to take a year and reach for the stars. "The best way to grow is to try and pursue something like that. I pictured myself sitting in a rocking chair when I was eighty years old, reflecting back on my life, and I didn't want to regret not having done something. I wasn't a wild success story, but I was able to go up there and send some money home to my parents and buy a car and pay for some of my tuition. I wouldn't discourage anyone from my background from trying to do the same thing," she said.

"It's funny now when I run into some of my old sorority sisters. Word's gotten around school, and a lot of people know who I am. I think people feel intimidated by me, and it's so ironic."

MASA KENNEY

Moultrie, Georgia

UNIVERSITY OF GEORGIA '96

During his teenage years, Masa Kenney cultivated his love for the thrill of the chase. "When we were growing up, we'd go out on camping trips and play paintball and war games and things like that. I don't know if it got into my blood or what, but it was pretty fun," he said.

Masa's middle brother decided to take the war games to another level when he joined the army right out of high school. "When I saw what he was getting—about $23,000 to apply to his college tuition for three years in the service—I thought that was a good deal.

"I've always been really independent. I didn't want my tuition to be a burden to my parents. My oldest brother ended up transferring to Emory, and that's one of the most expensive colleges in the country. My dad was having a hard time, always loaning him money. I could see myself getting into a bad situation with it, so I just decided to pay my own way through," he explained.

Masa followed in his middle brother's footsteps and opted

for a two-year enlistment in the army. "That's basically the lowest amount of time you can get. I just wanted to go in, get the experience, and get out. For two years, I got about $18,000 to put toward college," he said.

Though he was recruited in Georgia, Masa was pleased to discover that his destination was at least partly up to him. "It kind of surprised me how everything went. I wanted to travel the world, so I asked for a posting in Europe, and I was able to do it," he said.

Not, however, before he completed eight weeks of basic training under a drill sergeant's watchful eye. "You know all those movies you see? Well, I'd seen them, too. Basically, everything is true, but unless you've actually been through it, I don't think you could understand," he explained.

"He started cussing at us right away, just giving us the full-force shock treatment. You get that adrenaline rush for the first time, and everything moves really fast. You don't know what's going on. It takes a while to adjust to that level."

Masa did his basic training in Georgia. "The first thing we did once we got there was get in shape. You're going from 5 a.m. until 11 a.m. Calisthenics, marching seven miles with a fifty-pound pack. It's a shock to the system. I've never fallen asleep standing up before," he said.

The level of pain and suffering that the "cherries," as they are referred to around the army base, must endure is largely up to each unit's drill sergeant.

"They have a basic outline of the program, but they can do little things, too. If they catch you without your weapon, they can smoke you—make you do sit-ups and push-ups until you drop. Our drill sergeant made us eat with a spoon. I've eaten salads with just a big spoon. The other thing is, you always had to be done eating before he was. I've eaten entire meals in about a minute."

In the eight weeks of basic training and the optional six-week infantry training that followed, Masa learned the basics of weaponry and some specialized military strategy. "You learn how to throw a grenade, lay out land mines, defuse a mine, receive artillery, read a compass, use a topographical map, and navigate at night. There's a lot that goes into it to get your mind into a total state of awareness and caution."

Naturally, Masa wondered whether he would ever experience combat. "I was actually kind of hoping that I would. You get into a state of mind as to why you're going through this. It's not brainwashing, but it is hammered into your head over and over: It's either kill or be killed. Kill the enemy before he kills you. One shot, one kill," he said.

After his training, Masa was shipped off to a base in Mainz, a town on the Rhine River in southern Germany, where he would be stationed for the next year.

"If you're not in the war, you're training for it. That's all you do when you're in the army. We trained for different situations, different terrain. I rode in a tank and trained in these armored box-like vehicles that they used in Vietnam. We called them aluminum coffins," he said.

Once a soldier finishes basic training, the army becomes more like a nine-to-five job. Masa took advantage of the milder routine to soak up some European culture. "I traveled to Paris and Bavaria. I got to go to a ballet, and I saw some of Marc Chagall's work. I got to experience a lot of things I'd never have the chance to do in the States," he said.

He was also able to strike up a friendship with some Germans, especially those who shared his fondness for sampling the local brews in pubs near the base. "I fell in love with that beer. They really know how to party over there, and I quickly found out how alike we all are, no matter what culture we're from.

"Some things are very different, too. The Germans really look down on violence. A lot of the younger people did not like American soldiers at all. But with the older people, you still get the feeling that you're welcome there and that they remember what we did to help them rebuild after World War II."

After one year in Germany, Masa was preparing to return to the States to finish his tour of duty. Everything changed, however, when Saddam Hussein's forces invaded Kuwait and George Bush ordered them out by January 15, 1991.

"Basically, as soon as they changed my plans and told me I would be staying on in a different unit, I knew I would be going to the Middle East if there was a war. It was hard, though, because it was difficult to get information. Once a base was put on alert that they would be going to the Middle East, they couldn't make any outgoing calls. There's a real tight lid on security," he said.

"Lots of things were going through my mind while we were waiting to be put on alert—my family, my country. I knew I might die. I was calling my parents and my girlfriend, not trying to lay a sob story on them or anything, but just to say goodbye. I just didn't know whether I would be coming back or not."

Masa said that he wasn't aware of the controversy that was raging at home over the war. "In the army newspaper, they made Saddam out to be Hitler—a dictator. If I had known about some of the political aspects and the oil money, I might have been more against it. But I didn't understand any of that.

"All they told us was that this big country had invaded this little country and that our job was to go in and kick the big country's ass. I didn't have any doubts. Basically, I was being sent in to do what I was trained to do, and that's what I wanted to do. I was in a state of mind where I was going to go in and shoot a little girl if I had to, if I thought she was carrying a hand grenade behind her back," he said.

Masa's unit was the last one to land in Saudi Arabia before the air war began. "When the Scuds first started flying around, we had been sitting, about five hundred of us, in this huge warehouse. Outside, all of a sudden, we saw this yellow streak flying across the sky. When we went out to look, we saw a red streak flying in from the other direction to meet it, a Patriot missile.

"Everyone had to get back in to throw on mop gear in case they were using chemical weapons. When the Patriot took it out, there was a huge boom, and all this screaming. The explosion was so huge that these enormous ships in port started banging against one another because of the waves that the boom caused. It was the first big shock I had while I was over there," he said.

When the ground war began, there were other surprises. Masa had hoped to fight with his entire military unit intact. Instead, he was assigned to the dieseling unit. "That was the lifeline out there. Nobody could go anywhere without diesel, so I ended up riding this huge fuel tank. It was basically a time bomb.

"We advanced with the front lines, so we could see everything that was going on. We moved forward deep into Iraq to cut off their retreating lines. That's when I started seeing all the action—the wreckage, the fires, the bodies everywhere. We basically pulverized them," he said.

After the war, Masa's division got assigned to clean-up duty. "We were the last group in, so we had to stay. They had evacuated all these civilians because of the oil fires, and I ended up being stationed there for six weeks. The conditions were so bad that it would be dark in the middle of the day, and when it rained, you could see the soot on your arms."

After several more months in Germany, Masa returned to the United States and graduated from the University of Georgia in 1996 with a degree in landscape design. Like many veterans of the war against Iraq, Masa has experienced several symptoms of Gulf War Syndrome. "The fires, maybe in combination with some of the inoculations they gave us, that's supposedly what caused it. It's everything from nervous twitches to diarrhea and nausea. The problem is, the symptoms are not specific enough to really pinpoint any source. I've had a lot of trouble since then. I've made at least six trips to the Veterans Administration Hospital, but they're basically saying that I'm all right.

"I know my body, and I know if something is wrong with it or if it's changed. I'm basically in a situation now where I may not be able to have children, or they may be deformed. And the government still hasn't taken responsibility for what's occurring. They sent hundreds of thousands of people over there, and I think their biggest fear is having to pay out money to all these people."

TRACY JOHNSTON

Cold Spring, New York
WELLESLEY COLLEGE '95

Tracy Johnston was less than two months into her first semester at Wellesley College when she first heard The Voice.

"I was involved in College Democrats at the time, and we were in the living room watching the New Hampshire Democratic Convention. And there was Paul Tsongas and all the others and it was looking like a pitiful field," she recalled.

"And then I heard the voice, that unmistakable voice, and he had taken his coat off because he was all pissed and hot, and he was going on about how awful it is that there are all these people who don't have health care in this country. And I said to myself, 'Who is this guy?' "

When Tracy first laid eyes on that televised image of Bill Clinton in October 1991, he had almost no national name recognition, but thanks to a legion of true believers like Tracy, that soon changed.

"The next weekend I drove up to his campaign office, which had just opened, and I sat there and read about him for hours. Finally, I said to Chris, this twenty-two-year-old kid who was running the office at the time, 'I'm completely in. I am in love with this man.' "

Chris tried to convince Tracy to join the campaign right then and there, but she resisted. She had already taken one year off after graduating from the Hackley School in Rye, New York, and she didn't want to pack up and leave again. Yet.

"When I told Chris that I wasn't quite ready to drop out of Wellesley in the middle of my first semester, he didn't push me, but he said that before I made up my mind for sure, I had to at least hear Clinton speak.

"So when he spoke at the University of New Hampshire, I brought about ten people up. He just glided into the room, and everyone was silent. I was floored. He was the first politician I had ever heard who seemed personally to understand the value of a good education. He talked about lots of things that I really believed in, and then he started talking about the national service program. Our eyes locked for a moment. I started to cry, and instantly there was a connection.

"After that, I had a very hard time concentrating on college. This campaign seemed like the most important thing in the world to me then. I called up my parents and I said, 'You're not going to believe this, but I just met this guy who is going to be President.' They just started getting gray hairs again. I don't do things the easy way.

"I started going up to New Hampshire every weekend. I was so drawn to that life, and I felt that I needed to see what it was like without school hanging over my head."

On January 3, 1992, Tracy moved to New Hampshire to spend her winter vacation working full-time for the campaign. "I lived in Manchester, New Hampshire, in the Clinton hotel. It used to be a hotel or a dorm or something, and there were fifteen of us there during the week. But during the weekends it would swell to three hundred, even though the house only held fifty. So people were all over the floors and the beds.

"We would get up at six or seven every morning and spread out to these little towns all over the state to knock on doors and distribute literature, and then at eleven at night we would all come back and crowd around the television to watch the news and talk politics.

"My three weeks ended, and they asked me to organize Hillary's speech at Wellesley [Hillary Clinton is a Wellesley alumna]. Some of my friends from New Hampshire had already made the decision to leave school. I was toying with the idea, but I wanted to be really sure, so I came back and signed up for classes.

"My first day of classes, I was in physics, listening half-heartedly and writing notes about what I needed to do for the Hillary event. The semester before, I had been so excited about my classes, even when I was working on the campaign, and I realized that something really bad was going on.

"I called my parents right after class, and I told them that I had just sat through a class and not absorbed a word of what the professor was saying. My mother listened to everything, and then she said, and I'll never forget this, 'I don't ever want you to be somewhere and wishing you were somewhere else.'

"My parents came up for Hillary's speech, and it was an absolutely huge success, the best speech I had ever heard anyone give. The place was packed, and it was on the front page of every newspaper. She spoke about her generation, how they lived through the seventies and the greed of the eighties, and how it was their turn now. Their turn to take responsibility for the country and to fix things.

"When we were in private afterwards, she started to cry, and she said, 'Thank you, thank you for this day. I really needed to be here today and be reminded that some people still believe in what we are trying to do.' And she looked at me, and I told her that I had decided to leave school to come help them do this, and she said, 'You know, we're trying to fix education here. Bill will be unhappy.' "

But Hillary didn't forbid her to join the campaign, and the next day Tracy and her parents negotiated a tuition refund from Wellesley.

Tracy then returned to New Hampshire. "I worked in the field office all the way through to the end of the primary. We were doing basic grass-roots stuff. We were getting people out to hold signs, organizing walking routes for the weekend volunteers, sending out videos of Clinton. People used to be able to name voters in Concord, and I could tell them what street they lived on, what ward they were in, and who they were leaning toward. We were seriously after every single vote.

"The night of the primary was incredible. If we had had another two days, he would have won. That night, he gathered all of us and told us, 'No matter where you go from here, if you go home or if you come to Maine with us, you should never forget what we came here to do.' It got real quiet, and then everyone started to chant, 'We won't forget, we won't forget,' and he leaned forward, came off the platform, and hugged everyone there."

To recover from all the last-minute New Hampshire campaigning, Tracy slept for two straight days. She then hit the road to manage field offices in Maine, Maryland, Michigan, and New York. The other Democratic candidates dropped out one by one, until only Jerry Brown was left. Tracy said that she was sure from day one that Clinton would surmount the odds that were stacked against him, but she did have one fleeting moment of doubt in New York.

"There was a paid Brown staffer in the audience one night trying to get Clinton to say that Bush was a racist for vetoing the Civil Rights Act. When Clinton refused, the staffer tore up a Clinton campaign sign in front of all the television cameras there. So the speech had been great, the crowd was enormous, and there was their shot for the news: the tearing up of our sign.

"I was standing there afterwards with another person from the campaign, and we were both crying. How could we get the message out if we couldn't even keep Jerry Brown from orchestrating something like this?

"That moment of doubt lasted about five seconds, because Clinton saw us standing there, and he put a hand on each of our shoulders. We looked up at him, these two teary-eyed kids, and he said, 'It's going to be all right,' and I'm telling you, he was in great spirits, because he knew that it really was going to be all right. That was my one lapse."

After Clinton amassed enough delegates to clinch the nomination, Tracy wasn't sure what to do next. "Toward the middle of April, I called Chris, who by then was handling all the money for scheduling and advance workers at campaign headquarters in Little Rock, and he needed an assistant. [The advance people are in charge of doing everything possible to make the candidates look good on television and ensure that their public appearances go smoothly.] They flew me down, and a few days after I got there, he was promoted, and I took over his job," she said.

"So I was the money chick, just this kid running around to all these departments, trying to make sure there was enough money to cover the expenses of all the people out on the campaign who were doing advance work. Between me and the deputy director of advance, we were responsible for a staff of a hundred and twenty," she said. "I learned a lot about interoffice politics. We were in the tiniest office at first. We had this T-shaped table with all these people crammed around it. I had this little corner, with my calculator and my phone and all these binders, and I had to climb over the table half the time to get out."

The campaign paid her $1,000 a month, which she said was enough to live in a shared apartment in Little Rock. There was just enough left over for some good Southern barbecue and nightly forays to local bars for a little tension release.

"We would work from 7 a.m. till 11 p.m. every day and be so wired by the end that we couldn't go to sleep. So we would go out for food and beer, dance for a couple of hours, and then go back to our apartment to sleep before we started all over again the next day," Tracy said.

After two months of number crunching, Tracy had an epiphany. "It was July almost, and once again I had to decide whether or not I would be going to college the next semester. One day, I was sitting at my orange Sears desk, with one phone on my shoulder and one at my ear, and I had my calculator going and all these receipts, and all of a sudden I realized that I was an accountant.

"So I said to Stephen, the guy next to me, 'I'm an accountant. What am I doing with a desk job? I like science, not working at a desk.' So I went outside and took a walk, and when I came back, he asked me if I was all right. 'Yes,' I said, 'but only for Bill Clinton would I do this shit.' "

"It was so exciting to be a part of it, but what I eventually realized was that he didn't need me to get elected. In New Hampshire, it felt as if he needed every one of us giving everything we could to get him elected, but I no longer felt needed. This was not a local thing anymore, this was serious. It couldn't be as informal as it was in New Hampshire— otherwise, he would have lost. But it was no longer as much fun."

After making the decision to return to school, Tracy went

to the Democratic National Convention. "We flew into New York and landed at about eleven o'clock at night. I was carrying a suitcase with about $200,000 in campaign checks, $50,000 in paychecks, and $30,000 in traveler's checks, all to be delivered to advance staff and various campaign people. It was really heavy."

Tracy enjoyed every minute of the convention. "It was the biggest party I had ever been to, that is, until election night, and then until the inauguration," she said.

Though Tracy made two long weekends out of her trip to Little Rock for the election celebration and to Washington, D.C., for the inauguration, the convention was her last campaign hurrah, and she returned to Wellesley in September.

She threw herself into school with the same fervor that marked her stay in Little Rock. "I became this pumping student. I was taking five classes and three labs, and I set out to get a 4.0 and I did it. I have become incredibly focused and efficient, and I completely credit that to my having taken time off," she said.

"I always felt that when I was in college I wanted to be learning a lot in school, so that's what I do. My friends from the campaign call and don't understand the names of the classes I'm taking. They are still amazed that I made it back here."

Tracy graduated from Wellesley and in 1995 was awarded a Rhodes Scholarship, just as Bill Clinton was almost thirty years ago. She will finish her two years of study at Oxford in 1997.

PRISCILLA VAZQUEZ

Wenatchee, Washington

UNIVERSITY OF WASHINGTON '96

While preparing to graduate as a member of the Wenatchee High School Class of 1987, Priscilla Vazquez waited anxiously for her letter from the University of Washington, hoping she would be the first person in her family to attend college. When the acceptance letter arrived, she was overjoyed.

"Then I got a letter from the financial-aid office explaining my aid package," she said, "and I knew there was no way I could afford to go."

The University of Washington did not have any grant money to give Priscilla. It offered her only a small loan and expected her family to come up with the rest. "My family was making enough money to get by, but not enough to pay that much for me to go to school," she said.

She called the financial-aid office for advice. They told Priscilla that prospective students seeking more financial aid are eligible only if they have lived apart from their parents for a minimum of two years. During that time, their parents cannot have claimed them as a dependent on the family's tax forms. "I realized, 'Okay, in order to afford college, I'm going to need to take some time off, work, become financially independent from my parents, and then reapply to school,' " she recalled.

Priscilla made moving to Seattle and finding a job her first goal. "I called up a cousin there and said, 'Will you let me stay with you for a month while I get my feet on the ground?' I didn't want to become a deadbeat living off somebody, but I needed a boost to get started. I had a specific goal, and I allowed myself one month. He told me, 'That's what family is for.' "

Within a month, Priscilla found work as a cashier at a fast-food restaurant and moved into a cheap apartment in inner-city Seattle. "I was living in a rank, cockroach-infested building with a lot of strange people," she recalled.

She also signed up for a government-sponsored job-training program in the city. "I was studying to become a secretary or a receptionist. I got up at 6 a.m. for a long commute to school, finished class at 2 p.m., started work at three, got off my shift at 11 p.m., and then I came back home and collapsed."

But Priscilla's job as a cashier was not paying enough for her to make ends meet. "Five dollars an hour is really not very much money. I went to the landlord of my building and said, 'Look, I really need to stay here. Is there anything that I can do in the apartment building as janitorial work?' "

The landlord agreed to allow Priscilla to work thirty hours a month and deduct from her rent the wages she would have earned. "That was the worst job in the world," she said. "I don't even want to describe it. It was simply something that I had to do if I wanted to survive."

The building was populated by welfare recipients, elderly people, and the occasional drug dealer. "There were also a lot of really nice people, people who were struggling and that was the only place they could afford," she said.

Priscilla met an older man in the building whose health was failing. "He couldn't walk much or even make it to the grocery store very easily," she said. Priscilla began to drop by once a day to say hello.

"One day he asked me if I wanted to make some extra money by running errands for him," she said. "I told him I needed all the help I could get. I ran errands, helped clean his apartment, and had dinner with him once a week. He turned out to be a really nice old man. It was a good experience because I think we both were able to help each other."

Priscilla looks back on the period immediately after high school as one of the most difficult times of her life. Seeing so many people around her living in poverty also made a strong impression on her. "I did everything and anything that I could besides standing on a corner to survive," she explained. "I realized I didn't want to end up having to struggle for the rest of my life."

The job-training program was designed to last six months. Priscilla finished it in four. "They taught me about different filing systems and word-processing programs. I also learned to type quickly, take dictation, answer the phone in an office setting, and write proper business letters," she said.

The program helped Priscilla find employment as a secretary with a small company. "I finally got a good job," she said. "I was nineteen years old, living on my own, and making $15,000 a year."

The new job enabled her to move into a slightly nicer building. A few years later she began to think about going back to school.

Priscilla reapplied to the University of Washington and was

accepted. She also qualified for additional financial aid because she had been independent from her parents for more than two years. In the fall of 1990, more than three years after she had graduated from high school, Priscilla was back in school.

"I was working full-time during the day as a secretary and going to school full-time at night," she said.

Adjusting to the rigor of university-level academics proved to be difficult at first. "After I handed in the first paper for my English composition class, the teacher came to me and said, 'You know, I think you need to drop the class. Your writing skills are not up to par.' "

Priscilla explained to the teacher that she needed to stay in the class in order to earn enough credits to qualify for financial aid. "I told her, 'I'm going to prove to you that I can do this.' I also told her I was studying and working full-time." The teacher agreed to give Priscilla a chance and she ended up with an A in the class.

Despite that success, juggling work and school was difficult. "I was staying up late studying, going to work early, and having a hard time concentrating in class and on the job because I was so tired," she said. "My grades and my work were suffering."

Priscilla elected to pursue an anthropology major, a decision based in part on television shows she used to watch with her father. Her long-term goal is to become an archaeologist. "Deep down, I've always wanted to go on archaeological digs as a photographer for *National Geographic*," she said. "Watching nature shows as a kid made me want to discover things, to travel."

In the summer of 1992, Priscilla came upon her first opportunity to test out her interests. The archaeological field school of Washington State University was sponsoring a dig at a site located alongside the Snake River in Washington.

The group made some unexpected discoveries. "We were on a beautiful bluff overlooking the river," she said. "After digging for a while, we suddenly came across one skull and then another. It was a Native American burial site."

Priscilla threw herself into the experience. "My father came from Mexico as a migrant farm laborer and worked in the fields. Neither of my parents spoke proper English, but they taught me a lot about the importance of hard work," she said.

At the end of the summer, one of the professors approached Priscilla to thank her for her effort. Then he offered her a job. "He said, 'Well, we just got a contract in North Dakota for an exploration. We want to hire you for the project if you're willing to take time off from school for a semester.'"

Priscilla had promised herself that she would have a B.A. by the time her high school class met for their ten-year reunion in 1997. "I knew I was ultimately going to finish school, so I felt comfortable grabbing this opportunity," she said.

"We were in the Badlands, near some beautiful wavy, rolling hills. My job involved hard and tedious manual labor. I was shoveling, sifting, water screening, troweling, and pushing heavy wheelbarrows for long distances." Priscilla was also able to do some photography, a talent she was developing with her first job at *National Geographic* in mind.

When her job ended in October of 1992, Priscilla moved to California to live with one of her brothers. "I ended up working three jobs to make as much money as I could," she recalled. "I was working seven days a week, with an occasional day off."

Shortly thereafter, people from the dig in North Dakota called Priscilla to ask if she wanted to come back and work on the dig for the summer of 1993. After that dig, Priscilla made a difficult decision. "I was tired of working full-time and being a full-time student," she said. "Also, I had gotten myself into trouble with some credit-card debt and it was taking me too long to get myself out of it."

Priscilla decided going home to regroup made more sense than returning to school. "I wanted more financial stability," she said. "My goal was to be able to study at a university and only need to work part-time. Working more than twenty hours a week was just too hard."

Her parents welcomed her with open arms. "They didn't want me to leave in the first place," she said.

Priscilla's brother ran a janitorial service, and he agreed to let her work for the company. Meanwhile, living at home rent-free allowed Priscilla to pay off some of her debt and save money for school. She also decided to enroll at a local community college where the tuition was much cheaper than at the University of Washington.

Priscilla took some art classes, continued to work on her photography, and helped organize a gallery exhibit of students' artwork, including her own. In the spring of 1994, she graduated from Wenatchee Valley College with a two-year Associate of Arts degree.

After graduating, Priscilla applied to the University of Washington once more. She was accepted and enrolled in the fall of 1994. "I got my highest GPA ever those first two quarters," she said. Not having to work so many hours allowed her to make school her priority.

"To balance work and school, you have to know yourself," she said. "You have to know what you can take and what you can't take. And if you get put down once, get back up there and fight again."

In January, Priscilla sought out her academic advisor to see how close she was to graduating. "We went over my entire record," she recalled. "All my credits, my transfer credit, the classes I'd taken during the last two quarters, everything. 'You could graduate by the beginning of next year,' she told me. I was overwhelmed. 'Are you sure you're adding this up right?' I asked."

Priscilla was astounded to learn that she was so close to achieving her most important goal. "I realized I would need to set some new goals," she said.

Priscilla then remembered that most of the people running the archaeological digs she worked on had earned at least a master's degree, if not a Ph.D. She had her new goal. "I don't know how long it's going to take me, but I will have that Ph.D."

CATHERINE ULDRICH

Minneapolis, Minnesota

COLLEGE OF ST. BENEDICT, '90

When Catherine Uldrich arrived on campus in the fall of 1988 for her junior year of college, she found a surprise waiting in her mailbox.

"During registration, I received a letter saying I owed $2,500 to the college, money my dad had told me he was going to pay. He had broken promises before, but this one really hurt. The financial-aid officer basically told me, 'Sorry, you can't come here until you pay this.'"

Catherine felt angry and embarrassed all at once. "I wanted to call my dad up and say, 'Look, you fucker, you said you were going to do this and you didn't.'"

It had never been easy for her to confront her parents about difficult topics, however. Being raised in a family that struggled with depression and alcoholism gave Catherine a feeling of shame she found hard to shake off. Her parents divorced when she was thirteen and she remembers being told not to discuss it with anyone at school.

Matriculating at the College of St. Benedict, a women's

college in central Minnesota, was supposed to give Catherine a chance to escape some of the pressures she was feeling at home. "I really wanted people to know that I was normal. I loved college, because it gave me a chance to start all over."

Catherine had no way of knowing that she was going to have to start all over again twice. When she recovered from the surprise of the registrar's letter, she made up her mind to straighten things out on her own, instead of petitioning for more loans or other forms of assistance.

"I wanted to get away from St. Ben's and work to be able to stand on my own two feet. My mom was a big help at the time. I moved in with her and slept on the couch in her one-bedroom apartment. I got a full-time job teaching children to swim and working as a lifeguard at the YMCA," she said.

To deal with her growing depression, Catherine started going to therapy in the group known as Adult Children of Alcoholics. "Therapy helped me confront my feelings of shame. I learned to seek out people who love me for who I am and not for who I could be."

Looking through a newspaper one day, Catherine came across an ad announcing auditions for *The Miracle Worker*, a play about Helen Keller. In the beginning of her sophomore year, Catherine had registered for an acting class that was notoriously difficult. Doing well in the class and overhearing a chance conversation inspired her to continue experimenting with her interest in drama.

"I heard the professor talking to a male student in the class. He told him, 'I think you're very talented and you've got what it takes. You should audition for the spring play and sign up for the next level of classes." Catherine did just that, winning her first role in a dramatic production and settling upon theater as an area of academic concentration.

She tried out for the part of Annie Sullivan, Helen Keller's teacher, and landed her first role in a professional theater production. "Having a low-key job at the YMCA gave me a perfect chance to throw myself into the production. There were intense fight scenes where I would be forcing food into the mouth of the eight-year-old girl who was playing Helen Keller. The night my brother came to the theater, the girl got carried away and hit me hard in the mouth. He said afterwards, 'Oooh, that fight looked so real.' 'It was,' I said. 'She chipped my tooth.' "

By the time January rolled around, living at home rent-free had enabled Catherine to earn the $2,500 she needed to return to school. By adding extra credits during her remaining semesters, she was able to graduate on time with her classmates in the spring of 1990.

Her time away made Catherine more self-confident. "I came back to St. Ben's a much stronger person," she said, "and I was no longer afraid to speak out about the things that upset me."

Five days after she graduated, Catherine found herself in the islands of Micronesia training for a two-year position with the Peace Corps. "I was ready to spread my wings and fly. Joining the Peace Corps was a big risk for me and I was excited by the challenge." Unfortunately, she was struck with viral dysentery and had to come home early. "It was pretty hellish," she said.

Catherine returned to the United States and decided that what she really wanted to do was pursue her interest in acting. She worked as a nanny to save money for graduate school in theater and, in the fall of 1991, began the Master of Fine Arts program in drama at the University of Texas in Austin. Three years and tens of thousands of dollars later, Catherine had her MFA.

"All I want to do in my life is be an actor, but I am glad

my MFA degree will give me the safety net of working as a teacher as well," she said. She is auditioning for a variety of roles in productions around the country and has a job to help her pay the bills.

Sometimes Catherine finds herself feeling worried about the amount of her debt. "I'm part of the nouveau poor," she said, but she is confident she will be able to pay all her loans.

Catherine said her time off made her more aware of the importance of talking openly with people about their hardships and challenges. "Life is hard for everybody. I wish people would dump any sense of shame they have about what has happened in their lives. Divorce is nothing to be ashamed of, depression is nothing to be ashamed of, falling in love with someone and obsessing over them is nothing to be ashamed of.

"If you think that leaving school is not an honorable thing to do, or if you are embarrassed that you can't afford to pay for school right now, the best thing you can do is take responsibility for yourself. Stand on your own two feet and do what **you** have to do.'

PART TWO

Going Abroad

The more you know about a country ahead of time, the more successful you are likely to be when traveling, studying, or seeking employment there. Go to the library and check out some of the books they have about France. Look up Chile in the *Reader's Guide to Periodical Literature* and read some recent articles. Contact the Australian Embassy and ask them to send you all their informational brochures on traveling and working in Australia. Find the best bookstore in town—preferably a travel bookstore—and browse through the section on Kenya. Try to meet Japanese students at schools near you, and ask them for advice.

Don't leave home without an American Express card. They have travel offices all over the world where you can pick up your mail. They will hold your letters until you arrive, and if you ask them to, they will send them along to the next city on your itinerary. American Express offices are also a good place for you to change money. Your card enables you to write personal checks from your bank account back home in exchange for traveler's checks. You can do the same thing with a Visa card at certain banks. If you get in a pinch, you can have someone back home deposit a check in your account. If you don't have an American Express card, you also can have mail sent to you care of General Delivery at the main post office in the cities you visit. All you need to do is go to the post office and ask the clerk whether anything has arrived in your name.

Being able to get American cash dollars in another country is great, especially when you can get a better exchange rate by trading them for local currency on the black market. While exchanging money on the black market is always illegal and often dangerous, the practice in some countries is so common as to be akin to jaywalking. Traveler's checks don't work very well on the black market. Also, change only a little bit of money at a time, especially if you're somewhere with either hyperinflation or a lot of crime.

You will also want to look into getting some kind of insurance for yourself. Many insurance plans facilitated by schools will not cover you. Check with your family and your school to see if provisions can be made to insure you during your time off.

Youth hostels are often the easiest and most affordable places to stay when you first arrive in a new country. Most hostels require a membership card issued by the International Youth Hostel Federation. You can obtain a card by writing to IYHF (see page 263). Other hostel dwellers may be just like you—new in town and looking for a more permanent place to live. To find that place, you can start by posting flyers on bulletin boards in local coffee shops, bookstores, and college campuses. Many foreign cities have thriving communities of Americans, often with their own bars, churches, and English-language newspapers that include classified ads. You may be able to find an apartment by placing your own ad or visiting the local hangouts. You also could place flyers in residential mailboxes asking if people have a spare room to rent.

Working Abroad

Finding employment in a foreign country takes some legwork, but it can be done. Start by contacting the embassy in Washington, D.C., or the nearest consulate of the country in which you wish to work. Ask them about obtaining visas and work permits. Countries often have restrictions on the amount of work and the types of jobs open to foreigners; it's a good idea to find out ahead of time what the rules are. Many embassies and consulates have their country's Yellow Pages available. If you are interested in a particular area, say temporary work or language schools, ask them if you can photocopy those pages. Or you can check want ads in the country's newspapers, available in some libraries or at a specialty newspaper stand. When writing ahead to inquire about employment opportunities, be sure to enclose at least two international postal reply coupons, which are available at any post office.

Before you leave, do some networking. Tell everyone you know or meet where you are headed. Chances are, one of them will know someone in or near your destination. Keep a running list of names and telephone numbers, and then try to get in touch with these people when you arrive overseas. Even if they don't open their homes to you or offer you a job, they may be able to help you in unexpected ways. Most jobs available to young people without a particular skill will be relatively low-paying. Because your salary may cover only basic living expenses, it makes sense to find the most economical way to travel. A good travel agent, especially one who is used to students traveling on the cheap, can help you sort out the hype. Council Travel, with offices in dozens of cities and college towns, specializes in arranging low-cost air and rail travel. They can also help you obtain an International Student Identity Card. The ISIC entitles you to substantial discounts on transportation, accommodations, and admission to museums, theaters, and tourist attractions. As a general rule, cheap tickets come with many restrictions, so you need to consider how flexible your travel dates are.

KRISTIN WALKER

Alexandria, Virginia

SWARTHMORE COLLEGE '97

Kristin Walker's journey from Virginia to Vienna began when she was leafing through titles in a used-book store during her senior year of high school. "I like to go to bookstores and look at old books. I happened to come across one about finding jobs overseas in Europe, and I bought it on a whim," she recalled.

At the time, Kristin had been accepted at Swarthmore College and received permission to defer her matriculation for one year. "My whole life, people like my mother always promised me, 'Oh, when you get to junior high you'll like school better.' And then, 'Oh, when you get to high school you'll like that better.' And I never did. I didn't believe anyone who told me that when I got to college it would be different and that everything would be better."

Kristin's used book included the address of an au pair agency in Vienna, and she wrote to ask for the necessary application forms.

Paperwork was not her only obstacle, however. "When I

told one of my teachers, he said, 'Just don't get married and have kids. That happened to a niece of mine.' He thought I was going to Austria to get married to a rich baron or something. My English teacher said the same thing. It was ridiculous."

Additional resistance came from people in her community who were mystified by the idea of taking time off. "Many of the people in my town are lawyers and government people. They are very in to getting ahead on the fast track. To them, taking a year off means you lose a potential year of making money. And why on earth would anyone want to do that? Thankfully, my parents were very supportive of my idea."

The au pair agency Kristin wrote to placed her with a family in Vienna. Upon arrival, she was given a brief orientation by the agency and both she and her employers were required to sign a contract.

"The contract stated all the rules," she explained. "You are supposed to work five hours a day, six days a week. You must be given one day a week totally off. You must also be given your own private room and have your board provided for. The family is required to give you time to attend language classes if you want to. Finally, the family is to give you a weekly stipend, which for me amounted to roughly $70 per week. It's a great deal. Anyone can do what I did as an au pair. All they have to do is come up with the money for the plane ride over, which is not paid for."

Kristin was also expected to help with household chores. "One day I was working in the bathroom and I thought, I bet no one expected that Kristin National Merit Scholar Walker would end up scrubbing toilets in Austria. That's so great. I don't want to scrub toilets forever, but it wasn't bad for a year. You learn how to do it."

Kristin also learned to live on her own for the first time.

"Many au pairs live in the house with the family they work for, but I did not," she said. "I lived about a twenty-minute walk away in a room that belonged to a friend of theirs. I had a room, a toilet, and a sink in my room. And that was it, no fridge, no stove, nothing.

"The advantage was that when I was off at the end of the day I was really off," she recalled. "No one could say, 'Oh, could you watch the kids while I'm making dinner.' I had to go through two huge doors and up a flight of winding stairs to get to my rustic little room. I ended up loving it. I always felt like I was a starving artist living in a bohemian garret."

Kristin had the good fortune to be matched with a wonderful family. "I cannot say enough nice things about them," she said. "The mother, Eva, is a TV reporter for the Austrian Broadcasting System. She would always rush home because she wanted to watch herself on the news. The father, Stefan, works for the Green Party, and knows lots of important people. The Mayor of Vienna came over one afternoon for lunch.

"I hoped to really be treated like a member of the family, and I actually was. I became friends with the family's friends, met their relatives, went on vacation with them, was invited whenever they gave a party, and was generally treated with great kindness and respect."

Kristin's main responsibility was to pick up Phillipe from kindergarten every day at 2:30 p.m. and stay with him until his parents got home, which would be between five and seven. "When it was warm enough, we would go to the park. We spent a lot of time reading, playing games, and building with blocks.

"Phillipe and I had a schedule going, with lots of activities. On Mondays, I picked him up and brought him to a friend's house. There would be five or six little kids, and the music teacher would come. They all sat there and sang songs. I would sit with all the mothers and drink tea and argue about which was the best method to teach kids music. It was great for me to spend time with adults, mainly mothers in their thirties. I feel that I really learned a lot from them, and they treated me like an adult."

Kristin underestimated how hard it would be to take care of children. "Suddenly you're a mommy for five hours a day. It's very different from baby-sitting. You're not only responsible for making sure the kid doesn't get hurt. You have to learn how to discipline kids and teach them things. If you're depressed when the kid comes home from school, you're going to have to entertain him and make sure that he's okay. And if he misses his mother, you're going to have to comfort him, even if you miss yours."

Kristin's family was very happy to have her because their last three or four au pairs hadn't worked out. "They were interested in going to discos every night until 4 a.m. and drinking," she explained. "You can't party until 4 a.m. every night and be a good au pair in the morning."

In her spare time, Kristin pursued her goal of becoming fluent in German and learning more about opera. Being required to speak English with Phillipe made learning German more difficult. To learn faster, Kristin took German classes on Tuesday and Thursday mornings at the university.

"Classes were great," she recalled. "Most of the other students were also au pairs. Many were from former Communist countries, a lot were from the Netherlands. We had the most fascinating discussions. The woman from Russia would express her viewpoint, a woman from the Czech Republic would disagree, a woman from Norway would continue, and I would be called upon to express the American viewpoint."

During her year in Vienna, Kristin saw more than twenty operas. "This started as a minor interest and quickly became a passion of mine," she said. "Standing room at the Vienna State Opera costs $1.50. The first time, it was hard figuring out which line to stand in and where to go, but I soon became a pro."

Kristin loved waiting in line. "People wore everything from blue jeans to tuxedos. There were always a few people reading the libretto or studying the score and conducting the opera silently to themselves. I met the most interesting people: a man from Japan who was in Vienna for a human rights conference; an older Austrian man, dressed in a dapper gray suit, who lamented the new set for Wagner's *Ring*; an American woman on vacation; and a guy studying to be a doctor in Australia."

Kristin also took an opera class with friends who shared her enthusiasm. The group met at different people's houses and would watch a video of the opera they planned to see. They also studied the libretto and learned the basic musical themes. "The best part was when the teacher got opera singers to come and sing for us," she said. "It sounds absolutely incredible to hear an opera singer in someone's living room."

Kristin's advice to people considering working overseas as an au pair is to apply for a transfer if they don't get a good family. "You hear horror stories sometimes. Many au pairs come from former Communist countries in Eastern Europe and are there illegally. Some of the families look on them as cheap labor. People took advantage of some au pairs and had them work twelve-hour days, doing all the washing and ironing and sharing a room with the kids. A lot of bad situations can occur, like fathers that would make passes at the au pairs.

"Everyone should realize that they have a right to change families anytime. You can leave at any moment. If it's a bad situation, don't put up with it. Be assertive when you think people are treating you unfairly," she said.

Kristin suggests checking with the family ahead of time to

clarify expectations on both sides. "A prospective au pair should be able to find out what the job will be, the hours she'll be working, and where she'll be living. The more you can find out from the family beforehand about what you're going to be doing, the better off you're going to be," she said.

Kristin was originally anxious about making friends. "I thought it would be very hard to make friends, and actually it was not. The adults I met all treated me as an equal, which really meant a lot to me. I knew an opera singer, a math professor, a painter, a biologist, and lots of people from the foreign service. Austrians can be very private, but eventually I became friends with the neighbors and other Austrians my own age.

"In Austria, if I wanted friends, I had to go out and make them. If I was standing in line at the opera, and if I was feeling lonely and wanted to talk to someone, I would go up to people who were talking about something interesting and just sort of join in. You might have to give yourself a pep talk, but once you realize you can do it, it starts to build," she said.

"In high school, I felt like I had been put in such a pigeonhole. I had a role to fulfill as the good student, the good daughter, never staying out late or breaking the rules. In Austria, I could try new things.

"I also learned to drink. I never drank in high school and I was worried that everyone in college would be pressuring me to drink. Or that everyone would be drinking and that I wouldn't want to. There are no drinking-age laws in Europe and they have a more normal way of drinking. Nobody gets drunk at a party, they just enjoy a glass of wine and nobody makes a big deal of it."

Coming home was hard for Kristin. "I felt there wasn't anyone who was able to understand how much the experience had meant to me. When you come home, everyone expects you to be happy about coming home. You are, but there are still things you miss. I still feel homesick a lot for Vienna."

Kristin's attempts to introduce her friends to long afternoon chats over tea and evenings at the opera have met with mixed results. "I brought a tea set home with me. When I invited some friends over for tea, they said, 'Tea? I don't really like tea.' I said, 'Try it, you might like it.' They did and told me it was 'kind of yucky,' " she said.

When she began her freshman year at Swarthmore, Kristin started an opera club similar to the class she attended in Vienna. She has also been taking German literature classes.

"Going to Vienna to work as an au pair was by far the hardest thing I have ever done. I was homesick for the first three months. All of a sudden I was in a country where I knew absolutely no one and didn't speak the language very well. Sometimes I felt extremely lonely and tired of always having to make such an effort to say and do the simplest things. There were days when I woke up and felt like crying," she said.

"But throughout it all, no matter how depressed I was at times, whenever I asked myself the questions 'Is this worth it? Is this really what I want to be doing?' the answer was always yes."

TONI GOROG

Princeton, New Jersey

UNIVERSITY OF CALIFORNIA AT BERKELEY '94

Toni Gorog's infectious enthusiasm for science can catch people off-guard. Even Toni was not fully prepared for how far, literally, her passion could take her.

After graduating from high school in Princeton, New Jersey, Toni lived at home during the summer and fall while working at a deli. In January of 1990, she left for the University of California at Berkeley to begin college.

"Academically speaking, Berkeley was difficult. I had registered biology as my area of interest and was following their guidelines for course selection. I quickly learned what studying hard means."

In the fall of 1992, Toni finished what she called "those pain-in-the-butt lower-division courses full of pre-meds" that she was required to take. "It's stressful to be in a classroom with six hundred students where the competition is cutthroat. I was relieved to get into the upper-division classes specific to my major. There were some amazing and energetic professors who made those classes more interesting.

"My first good upper-division class was Comparative Animal Physiology. Then in the spring of 1993 I took the class that opened up a whole world of possibilities for me: Natural History of the Vertebrates. We studied birds, mammals, and reptiles and amphibians. During our in-class lab, we learned, by looking at animals and memorizing, how to tell different species apart, what they eat, where they live, and when they migrate. We also had field lab once a week. It was great because we actually got to see the Bay Area and visit different parks."

During the mammology section, the class did some live trapping. "The traps we used didn't hurt the animals. They walked in to get the bait, triggered a spring, and the door closed, so they were stuck inside. We then took the animal out and performed all the measurements, like weight, body length, ear length, and tail length. We also learned how to identify California species."

Toni's enthusiasm did not go unnoticed. "I would go out there all the time with my friend Rachel, who was also a student in the class. Sometimes we wouldn't take notes. We would just sit and watch the birds we were studying, because it was so fun. We started to get to know our TA, Albert, a grad student from Brazil who was working on his Ph.D."

Albert told Toni of his plans to return to Brazil in the summer of 1993 to do fieldwork for his dissertation on fruit bats. "I talked with Rachel and we said to ourselves, fieldwork in Brazil could be amazing. Let's ask Albert if he wants our help.

"One day we were hanging out with him at the end of a lab, and we said to him, 'By the way, do you think you would ever need any help?' Albert's response was 'Oh, I don't know, maybe.' A few weeks later, Albert came up to us and said, 'You know, I've been thinking about what you said, and I am going to need some help. If you want to, you can come.' We were stunned. We thought no, it's not going to happen. But it did.

"It turned out that Albert needed help during the fall semester of 1993. I decided, 'This experience will be so worthwhile. I'm going to go.' I owe it all to that class. I know that sounds cheesy, but it's true. There are well-known biologists who credit this class when they publish their papers: 'Yeah, I took IB 104 ten years ago and it's the reason I'm a biologist now.' "

Albert's advisor had another Brazilian grad student, Meika, who was also going back to Brazil at the same time to do her fieldwork. "So he asked us, 'Any chance that you want to help Meika also?' And we said, 'Sure, fine. You arrange it, we'll do it.' We sat and planned with Meika and Albert. But a lot of things were left unplanned. We weren't really sure exactly what was going to be happening in Brazil."

Toni was responsible only for her round-trip airfare, which she paid for out of her savings from previous jobs. Albert and Meika took care of all other essentials. "I didn't even borrow money from my parents, who supported the idea. They weren't worried that I was going to flake off and never come back to school. My friends were also excited for me.

"Rachel, Albert, Meika, and I met in São Paulo, Brazil, on September 1. Three of us took a bus to Paraná to pick up our car, a 1979 VW Bug. We would be driving along, come up over a hill, and find a huge bus in our lane barreling toward us. When Rachel came back to the U.S., she immediately got a ticket for driving too close behind someone else, because in Brazil you just follow right on their tail. It doesn't matter, there are no rules.

"The maldistribution of wealth in Brazil is staggering. Something like ninety percent of the wealth is owned by ten percent of the people. The city slums, called *favelas*, are terrible.

"The rain forests really are being destroyed. We did so much driving because the areas of primary forest are few and far between. Minas Gerais, a state in eastern Brazil, looked totally deforested. It was really sad."

There was no such thing as a typical day for Toni and her group. "Albert and Meika were doing similar research. They were trying to understand the diversification of species and explain the fragmentation of different groups of animals in the rain forest. The basic purpose of the project was to look at the geographical distribution of species and populations in order to uncover the history of the groups and the forests in which they lived. Studying those basic patterns lays a foundation for the sound management of biological diversity."

Albert was studying several groups of tropical fruit bats. "We were catching the bats with Japanese mist nets. People also use them for catching birds. You can stretch out the nets between trees or poles. They come in different lengths and they're about three to four meters high. They're made of really fine thread, and have little looped-down pockets. So if an animal flies into the net, it will drop into the pocket and get tangled up in it."

Meika was researching a group of small marsupials known as the mouse opossum, or *Marmosops*. "She was carrying 120 traps—eighty Shermans and forty Tomahawks. Shermans are made of either steel or aluminum. Tomahawks are bigger and they're made of wire. They are both live traps.

"Our objective was to collect tissue samples from the animals they were studying. Those samples were then brought back to be housed in a museum. Researchers can sequence parts of the DNA to study evolutionary relationships between groups of animals and can infer how long ago the divisions between them occurred.

"It was necessary to keep really good records of the localities we worked in and the measurements we took. I was constantly writing things down and taking notes. Our notes were bound and put into the museum collection for anyone who wants to use our work."

Toni's group traveled all around southeastern Brazil. "We'd usually arrive wherever we were going sometime in the afternoon. At about six in the evening, we would go and set out the mist nets. We couldn't open them before it was dark because then we'd end up catching birds instead of bats. We'd mist-net until about midnight, sometimes until one. And then we'd take the nets down and go to bed.

"We would usually wake up around seven, and if we had already set up Meika's traps, we would go out and check them. If not, we would go out and set them. We baited the traps with peanut butter and bananas.

"Usually, the first day there wouldn't be that much work. If we hadn't had time to mist-net the night before, we wouldn't have any samples to prepare, so we'd have some free time in the afternoon.

"First, we would measure the animal. Each bat gets a tag, from which you can tell species, sex, all the measurements we took, the locality, the altitude at which it was caught, the name of the collector, and the name of the person who prepared the specimen. The specimens are invaluable. They provide important information about reproduction, distribution, genetics, and morphology that is fundamental for conservation programs.

"It was hard even to find time to write in my journal, but I managed to do it. Luckily, there were a few times when we'd go on a hike to a waterfall and swim."

Toni worked in Brazil from September to December of 1993, and says she fell in love with the country. "Everywhere we went, I would say, 'Okay, you guys go on, I'm going to stay here.' I had just read García Márquez's *One Hundred Years of Solitude*. One afternoon, I came to a house that used to border a coffee plantation that had since vanished. It was just like the Buendías' house in the novel. I took a shower in a bathroom with huge windows facing this overflowing garden fading into a forest of purple flowers."

Toni got along well with her companions. "Everyone was really hardworking."

She also said the trip was an important confidence builder for her. "I have field experience that many grad students don't have. It's nice to be able to talk about what I've done and be able to understand what other people have been through. I never regretted devoting myself to school before, but after this, there's just no question in my mind. I'm completely into my studies.

"I used to get really caught up in school and in trying to do well. I would get bummed out when my grades weren't ideal. Now, having done this, I feel I might be good at what I do. I also know that being good at something isn't only a question of grades."

Toni has since graduated from Berkeley and is pursuing a Ph.D. in biology at the University of Michigan.

"If you want to do field research, the best thing is go around and talk to people. If there is someone who inspires you, go and talk to that person.

"After I had already gotten my job in Brazil, the professor took our class for pizza and beer after the last field trip. We were sitting around talking about our plans for Brazil. A woman named Sasha said, 'Wow, I'd love to find a field job like that.' The professor said, 'What's that, Sasha? You need a field job?' And he called over Sandra, one of the teaching assistants, and said, 'Sandra, do you need a field assistant for Samoa?' So Sasha went with Sandra to Samoa. As easy as that."

Studying Abroad

Most people who study abroad do it during their junior year of college. Those students generally enroll directly in a foreign university or participate in a program sponsored by an American school. Students who take time off to study abroad between high school and college face a similar set of options. Formal programs, while often expensive, make things easier for you by taking care of travel and housing arrangements, enrollment in school, and academic credit. By enrolling directly in a foreign university and finding a place to live on your own, however, you can often save thousands of dollars.

Carefully evaluating the foreign study programs you are considering can save you much aggravation later on. Where will you live? What kind of classes will you be taking, and who will the teachers be? Are foreign students a welcome presence at the school you will be attending? How old will the other participants be? What is and is not included in the fee you pay to the program? How much money will you need once you get there? The best approach is to ask the programs to supply you with a list of several past participants. Call them and ask for their honest impressions of their experience. Once you're on the program, don't be shy about speaking up if your expectations are not being met.

Students who try to get college credit for their time off often meet with resistance. After all, the vast majority of students pay tuition money for credit, so why should colleges give it to you for free? Many schools will also argue that experiential learning is not worthy of credit. Talk to a dean or the registrar before beginning your foreign study to find out if there is anything you can do to get credit for your time off.

CELIA QUEZADA

Gonzales, California

WILLIAMS COLLEGE '94

In the early 1960s, Celia Quezada's father left Mexico to work in the United States through the bracero program, an agreement between the United States and Mexico which brought Mexican guest workers into the U.S. for seasonal agricultural labor. "My father drove a tractor and my mother did jobs like hoeing weeds during the lettuce season, bunching onions, and packing tomatoes. When I was younger, I sometimes worked with my mom in the fields," she said.

Growing up, Celia felt caught between two cultures. The high cost of living in the United States during the months when her parents had no work would force her family to return temporarily to Mexico. "Every year during the rainy season, we would migrate back to Mexico. Even though our home was in the States, Mexico lived within me. Little kids used to hate me when I went back; they called me the gringa."

Just before beginning high school, Celia experienced what she views as her biggest break. "In eighth grade, I didn't know universities existed. I just knew that after high school I had to find a job somehow. I thought that maybe I could be a secretary for some lawyer," she said.

That summer, Celia went to a special seminar at the University of California at Santa Cruz known as the *Yo Puedo* program. "*Yo Puedo* is Spanish for 'I Can,' and it was part of a program conducted by the state of California for the children of migrant farm workers. It totally enlightened me. They taught me about financial aid and universities. They said I didn't have to stick to California. They made me believe that I could do it," she recalled.

"I went for all of it. In high school, I stuck my nose in everything. I wanted to change the world, I was Miss Gung-ho." Celia had to juggle her many extracurricular activities with responsibilities at home. "I'd get home at six, then I had to clean the house and cook because, if your mom is working, someone has to do it. You can't make her do everything. I wouldn't start studying until nine and then I'd go to bed around 2 a.m."

Celia was president of her school's student body. She felt that the majority of the students didn't care about the school's Spanish-speaking population. "Every time I took the microphone in front of people, I would translate. I noticed that every time we chose the staff member of the month, it was a teacher. I asked, 'What about the cafeteria workers, the bus drivers, the custodians? If they weren't here, who would be cleaning your toilets? It would be a pigsty.' So we acknowledged them. It's a question of treating people like people."

She was accepted at Williams, the first person in her family to attend college. Celia's parents fully supported her college plans, but they became apprehensive when she contemplated postponing her studies to spend a year in Europe with the Rotary Club's exchange program.

Celia made it to the final round in Rotary's application process and was then required to bring her parents in for an interview. "They asked my parents the question I'll never forget," Celia recalled. 'Do you realize you will not see your daughter for one entire year?' " Celia saw her parents' eyes begin to get teary. It seemed for a moment that they might not be willing to let her go. But: "Whatever's best for *mi hija*, my daughter," Celia's parents declared. "Whatever she decides."

Celia won a scholarship from Rotary, but instead of offering her one of the three countries she had listed on a preference questionnaire, they proposed to send her to Belgium. "I didn't even know Belgium existed," Celia said. "People would ask me, 'Haven't you heard of Belgian waffles? And Brussels sprouts?' "

After she graduated from high school, Celia went through some last-minute jitters. "I did not want to go," she explained. "What the hell was I going to do in Europe? I always thought that was for snobs."

Celia's anxieties worsened when her host family greeted her at the airport in Brussels. "They had a Jaguar, so immediately I was intimidated. Then I saw that all the taxis were Mercedes-Benzes or Volvos, and that some of the highway patrolmen drove Porsches. This, I thought to myself, is a wealthy country."

Celia had difficulty with her first host family, which added to the challenges of adjusting to life in a foreign country. "They would always speak English to me, so I couldn't learn Flemish," she said. "And the little girl was always shoving a dictionary at me and saying, 'Learn it! Learn it!' Then, to top it off, my host mother was reading my diary. So I wrote in my diary, 'I know she reads my diary and she's stupid for doing that.' "

Celia convinced Rotary to find her another family. She advises those who feel trapped in difficult situations to stick up for themselves. "Don't be afraid to say that something is making you uncomfortable or unhappy," she said. "If you're on a program and get assigned to a family that is not working out for you, ask to be switched if you're sure you have given it a fair chance."

Celia's second family turned out to be literally a second family to her. Her new host father announced that he didn't speak English very well and that Celia was going to have to learn Flemish. " 'That's why you're here,' " he told Celia. "I started speaking Flemish, and I became really close to the family. They ended up buying me a plane ticket so that I could go back and visit them a year later," she said.

Rotary arranged for Celia to enroll as a student at a local school. "It was a drag sometimes, not being able to understand what was going on in school. I ended up going to a fifth-grade French class. Sitting in the middle of all these kids, I thought to myself, 'At least I'm learning something.' I also went to Flemish night classes."

"I was so used to doing the right thing at home, but in Belgium I didn't know what the right thing was. The trick for me was being open-minded. You have to accept the culture the way it is."

Celia was in Belgium during the Persian Gulf War and found herself having to defend the United States. "Some people in Belgium were racist, and during the war there was a lot of anti-American feeling. Some thought that all Americans were fat and that we all eat hamburgers every day. One person told me that Americans were dumb for being patriotic. I said, 'If we're so dumb, how come we have many of the world's leading universities in America?' I told them that my parents left Mexico because their country couldn't offer them what the United States could."

Celia wanted to see some more of Europe while she was

there. Sometimes she was able to tag along with her host family for free. She also discovered a creative way to raise her own travel funds. "I cooked a huge Mexican meal for all the Rotary members. They paid me for everything I needed for the meal; they paid for my trip, and gave me a few hundred dollars' spending money," she said. Celia ultimately was able to visit Paris, London, Prague, and Vienna.

After her Rotary year was over, Celia returned home to California before starting Williams College.

"Taking time off was one of the most important things that ever happened to me," she said. "It took courage to stick it out and not give up. My parents instilled in me a drive to always do more, to not hang around in this measly little town of Gonzales. So even though I got to the point with my first host family where I felt like jumping out of my second-floor window, at least to break my leg so I could be sent home, I knew that coming home early would be letting everyone down. Once I made up my mind to stay and make the best of it, I found myself doing things that I would never have seen myself doing here. I became more independent. I think it really helped me grow.

"Taking time off also made me respect my parents even more than I did before. For all they went through, for all they struggled for. All I had ever really known was Gonzales, this small little town. It was great to see what it is like out there in the world. A lot of students who go straight to college don't even know what the heck the real world is. They've always been supported by Mommy and Daddy, who give them money and a pat on the back. 'Oh, here, honey, I found you a job.' Because everything has been given to them on a silver platter, they have no idea how the real world works."

After graduating from Williams, Celia wants to teach for a while and then pursue her interest in politics. "I want to go into education and I hope to promote multiculturalism. I recently had an argument with a woman who told me that since I had never learned about her and her culture, why should she have to learn about mine? I said, 'What do you think I've had to learn my whole life since kindergarten? I've been studying American culture.' California has so many different minorities, and the whole education system needs a lot of reforming," she said.

"I was very lucky because my parents emphasized education as a way to get ahead. My parents always tell me, 'Whatever is best for you, as long as you don't end up in the fields.' "

GEOFF NOER

Northfield, Minnesota

SWARTHMORE COLLEGE '95

Geoff Noer was raised to have a broad worldview. His mother is French Canadian, and his father, a physics professor at Carleton College in Northfield, Minnesota, used to pack the family off to Europe during his sabbaticals.

So when Geoff began his senior year of high school, he resolved to go where no Noer had gone before.

"Growing up in a college town is special. People tend to be a lot more open to the idea of doing something different. Every year, about six or eight kids from my high school went away for a year after they graduated," he said.

Even the free spirits from Northfield, however, generally chose fairly familiar locales. "I'd been in Switzerland, so Belgium or someplace like it wouldn't have been as new. Because I already knew that culture fairly well, it would have meant that I really would have been able to get into it and be fluent in French. But there's something to be said for getting an entirely new experience."

When Geoff applied to the Rotary program, he looked at the countries that were available and picked as his first choice the only place he had never heard of, the Faeroe Islands. The Faeroes apparently weren't that high up on anyone else's list, and Rotary agreed to send him there.

The Faeroes are hard to locate even in top-of-the-line *Rand McNally*s. Find Denmark and then look northwest and you'll see the islands just outside the Arctic Circle.

While the Faeroe Islands are part of Denmark, residents speak Faeroese, not Danish, which made it very hard for Geoff to prepare linguistically for the experience. "There was no way to learn the language ahead of time," he said.

When he arrived, he began the equivalent of senior year in high school, but just getting to class every morning presented a problem. "I lived on one island, took a ferry to another, and then took the bus. Sometimes I hitchhiked instead, which brought the commute down to about an hour or so."

And once he arrived, he found himself lost in his classes. "The teachers were mostly Danish, and they would ask questions in Danish, but the students would answer in Faeroese. I slowly picked up some Faeroese, but I didn't speak Danish and I still don't. Basically, I spent a lot of time just being bored."

Even though a few of the students spoke some English, Geoff avoided speaking his native language unless it was absolutely necessary. "I felt uncomfortable speaking English to Faeroese students. I wanted to fit in as fast as possible, because you can't completely understand the culture if you don't speak the language."

Geoff had trouble finding a comprehensible textbook. "The only thing I found was this book written by some Oxford professor for linguistics Ph.D. students. The book wasn't even written in a language that I could understand. It might as well have been written in Faeroese."

So Geoff made flash cards and spent a lot of time asking people to explain themselves. "I'm sure that got very tiring, but it gave me some clue. By the end of the year, I had some basic conversational ability. Even without knowing any grammar, you can throw words together and people may understand you," he said.

Without any other American students to count on for support, his lack of conversational ability combined with his classmates' spotty English made it difficult for Geoff to make friends quickly.

Geoff also had trouble bridging certain cultural gaps. "I think I spent too much time being conscious of the fact that everyone was stereotyping Americans based on the way I behaved. It's very easy to think that, because everyone is always watching you. You're the strange one there."

At the same time, Geoff worried that his levelheaded demeanor may have disappointed his peers and their active imaginations. "People expect you to act a certain way if you are an American. I didn't quite meet their expectations, since most of them seemed to come from television shows like *Dallas*," he said.

Residents of the islands tend to live fairly far apart, which also made establishing relationships very difficult. "When people live in small villages on different islands a couple of hours apart, you're not going to just drop by for a visit. Plus, it feels funny to walk into someone's house and say, 'Hi, can I intrude on you for a while,' though you almost have to do that in order to socialize," he explained.

Because there was so much about his experience that was new, he still has trouble making broad generalizations about it. Certain cultural traits were telling, however.

"One thing that struck me is how much closer people are to their food sources there. Regardless of what job you do, you are liable to own ten or fifteen sheep that mill around in your yard. One day, we took one down to the basement and slaughtered it. I took a lot of pictures.

"They also do a noncommercial pilot-whale hunt every year. They go out in large boats and form a wedge, driving the whale toward the shore until it's beached. I participated in one. Basically, they get the whale to the shore and then jump out and slit its throat. The whole bay turns bright red."

The hunt has been the target of numerous Greenpeace protests, which Geoff doesn't understand. "Look at how animals are raised in the U.S., cooped up in tiny pens. It's pretty horrid. In the Faeroes, the whale spends its whole life at sea and the death is fairly quick. Plus, it's a tradition, it's a part of life there, and every last bit gets eaten or used somehow."

A talented violin player, Geoff found many musical opportunities once he sought them out. "I had been worried about being able to continue to play, but the headmaster of my school was a violinist, and he arranged for an audition with the Faeroese National Symphony Orchestra. I ended up being first violin," he said.

After several weeks of school, Geoff had made little progress linguistically. Instead, he began skipping half days to make a three-hour commute to a music school run by the ex-concertmaster of the Copenhagen Symphony.

Music led to new friendships. "I think that probably helped the most. I got to know a trumpet player and someone who liked to play the guitar. We started playing improvisational music and folk songs in the street."

Geoff admitted that the isolation got to him. He was able to leave the islands only once, because it was so expensive to fly or even cruise to Scandinavia. When the days shortened to three or four hours in midwinter, he said, it was hard to avoid sinking into depression.

Geoff is proud of the way he grew. "It was a fascinating year, really, and it certainly had its high points. But there were a lot of low points, too. A year like this forces you to be completely independent. You learn how to be by yourself and deal with things."

BEN COOLIK

Columbus, Georgia

UNIVERSITY OF GEORGIA '98

Ben Coolik never doubted that he would spend a year in Israel between high school and college. His only problem was convincing everyone else.

Ben went to a private school in Columbus, Georgia, for thirteen years. "It was predominately white and Christian. Growing up, I participated in Young Judaea, a national youth movement that seeks to promote Israel. I went to camps and weekend programs, which was great for me, because I got to hang out with all these other Jewish kids.

"Young Judaea has a year-long course in Israel for about 150 people who have just graduated from high school. They're really big on their program, so Year Course is hammered into your head as you're growing up. By freshman year of high school, I knew I was going to do it," he said.

Ben's high school promoted a more traditional route. "Everyone was on the college track. Their college matriculation rate is a hundred percent, and their dropout rate is zero. They never mentioned time off. I don't think anyone had ever even thought of it.

"At first, I don't think they were too excited about me going. The biggest question was, how can we fix this where we have him graduating and going to college so we don't lose our hundred-percent rate in the national rankings. The alumni magazine came out when we graduated in the spring of 1993, and next to my name they wrote 'University of Georgia, Fall of 1994.' Not a word about me going to Israel," he recalled.

Ben's father was also skeptical, and it took an all-out lobbying effort to turn him around. "My dad said no when I was a freshman, no when I was a sophomore. Then, when I was a junior, he said, 'We'll see.' I started talking to people in the Young Judaea office to get them to talk to him about it, tell him success stories. I just worked him and worked him.

"His biggest problem? Whether I would ever come back —that I would want to stay forever or join the Israeli Army or something. There was also the wars, the propaganda on TV. He thought of Israel as some big desert battlefield. When he finally broke down, it wasn't even a breakdown, it was a complete change in position. He said, 'Ben, you are going to Israel. I have talked to so many people who told me what a great thing it is in so many ways that I wouldn't want you to do anything else at this point.'"

Ben's father also wanted him to go to college, preferably at his alma mater, the University of Georgia. Ben spent the summer after high school taking classes at the Columbus branch of the state university system so he could still graduate from college four years after he finished high school. Right after Labor Day, though, he packed his bags and drove to the Columbus airport.

"My dad was crying at the airport, and I felt bad, but it didn't really hit me until I got to Atlanta to change planes to fly to Kennedy in New York. Then I was flooded with all these emotions.

"I looked around the plane, realizing that I was going to be with strangers for an entire year, and I broke down in tears. The old lady sitting next to me asked me what was wrong, and I told her that I was leaving home to spend a year in Israel. Well, that's where she was going! So she starts telling me all these great things about how wonderful Israel is, how pretty the girls are. She just totally made me happy," he recalled.

When Ben arrived in New York, he met up with his group. There are three groups of American students on Year Course each year. The course is divided into different segments and is designed to give students as broad an exposure to Israeli life as possible.

Ben's group was a cross section of standard teenage stereotypes. "There was Ira from Texas, and all he talked about was hunting and his truck. There were a couple of deadheads with goatees and Afros. There were girls from New York who thought they were cool because they listened to Phish. There was one really rich guy from Beverly Hills. Then there was this guy from Miami who had all these crazy outfits and was really into bodybuilding."

After a brief orientation session in the airport, two counselors herded them onto their flight. "When we first got there, they had us all think for a few minutes about why we were there, just to get our minds set for the year. At that age, you're basically the sum of everything you've been taught. I wanted to find out more about what kind of person I was and what kind of personal goals I wanted to set for myself."

Like all Year Course groups, Ben's group started their year in Jerusalem with a week-long orientation. The group then headed North to Ma'alot, about twenty miles from the Lebanese border, where they spent ten weeks working.

Israeli development towns originally were built to help absorb new immigrants quickly. New arrivals could get housing easily, learn Hebrew, and receive instruction on finding employment and a permanent place to live. As Israel has grown, however, the area around the immigrant absorption center in Ma'alot has grown as well, and today it is a full-fledged town in its own right.

Ben's group lived in a small apartment in the absorption center and performed manual labor there in exchange for rent. Each student also had a community project, and Ben chose to volunteer in the local high school.

"I taught conversational English to eleventh- and twelfth-graders. We painted a bomb shelter in the high school and turned it into a classroom. The teachers would bring their students down, and they would ask us all sorts of questions about America."

Ben made friends with several of his students and spent weekends with them in their homes and in the local bar. "It was this small wooden place, and the bartender let us run a tab because we were all so broke. Ira would bring in Garth Brooks, and we would just listen to music and hang out."

For the first few weeks, Ben's group also spent three hours a day in an intensive Hebrew language class. "The language was a big obstacle in Ma'alot. It's not necessary to know the language in other parts of the country, but there they wanted us to get over it quickly," he said.

After a week-long hike in December, Ben's group spent three weeks on an Israeli Army base. "We had to wake up at 5:30, put on fatigues, do calisthenics, and eat in the mess hall. Some Israelis think it's bullshit—that we're just out there playing toy soldier while they're fighting to keep the country alive. But for us it was cool to see what life was like for kids our age who have to be in the army.

"We took it pretty seriously. They had this one tank storage room that they needed to tear down to make the tank fields bigger, so we were in there moving fifty-pound bales of barbed wire out," he said.

In January, Ben's group returned to Jerusalem for the academic portion of the program, which included more intensive Hebrew instruction, classes on Zionism and geography, and electives. Classes were graded, but a pass/fail option was available, and many students were able to obtain college credit for the courses when they returned to the States.

Ben and his group then traveled to the Golan Mountains in northeastern Israel to spend time on a moshav. Moshavim are planned communities where families farm their own land (as opposed to kibbutzim, where the land is communally owned) and meet collectively to address matters that affect everyone.

"A lot of people take advantage of that time to live with a family that doesn't speak English, so they can really work on their Hebrew. But part of the point also is to learn what it is like living with an Israeli family.

"I worked in the flower fields—on my hands and knees—for six hours every day. I also worked in the palmetto fields, picking off the rotten ones and setting rat poison. I got up really early, and it just felt so good. After work was done, we'd pick oranges and lemons and grapefruits off the trees and make these amazing juices," he said.

Ben noted that the sense of community on a moshav is incredibly strong. "I worked with the turkeys some, and they all got very sick while I was there. It was cool to watch everyone come together to figure out what was wrong and then to pitch in for vaccinations."

Most Young Judaea groups do a two-month stint on a kibbutz. Ben's did not, but he said it is possible to arrange for kibbutz stays of varying length.

Year Course participants also spend several weeks as volunteers in a profession of their choice. Ben decided to work in a theater in Jerusalem. "The options are endless, and Young Judaea will help you find something that interests you. I had done a lot of theater as a child, and I wanted to do some technical work. I started calling around, and one place said that it might have an opening. Their tech person had just quit, so I kept calling and calling and they finally gave me a job because I was so persistent.

"They had a real simple light board, and I repatched it. I worked hard at it, and they appreciated the fact that I was putting so much effort into something that I wasn't getting paid for. I did lights for the Friday-night jazz jam—Irish, Balkan, and flamenco music—and for a two-act play.

"I would work from six until midnight. Then I would clean up, go out until four in the morning, then sleep until four the next day. That was my life-style for six weeks. It was a really cool time.

"I've heard people say that it is hard to make it in Israel, but if you're American and you have some kind of skill or talent, it's so easy. They would have hired me for a paying job if I had been able to stay."

After a tearful weekend of goodbyes, Ben returned home to reflect a bit before starting school in the fall. "Israel was very much a cultural awakening for me. In America, we use religion as a basis of how Jewish we are. But when you're in Israel, it's the Jewish state, so you don't really have to prove your religiousness.

"There was a great guy in my group, Leore. He really used a lot of his brain, and he's the one that helped me realize that happiness is more important than money. He turned me on to different authors and the whole idea of the power of the individual.

"A lot of people come back from Israel even more religious than when they left, because they're trying to replace Israeli culture with something. I still feel very much culturally Jewish, but because of the philosophies I chose, I came to believe that we all have the ability to perform miracles, and less that God controls things.

"I was totally alone in a strange country. Having to worry about yourself—that's a tremendous responsibility, if you think about it. But that's the great thing about the program. You learn to handle that without getting bogged down by it," he added.

Ben maintained a perfect 4.0 during his first two quarters as a finance major at UGA. "Everybody here calls me Mr. Dad because they think I'm so responsible about everything. But during the first quarter my dad told me that I was studying too much. I mean, that was my **father** talking."

Ben's experiences in the theater had left an indelible mark on him as well. "I want to be studying theater, but there's not a lot of money in that, and I feel that I should have a backup. But finance—I just don't agree with everything I'm learning, all these limitations in economics and things like that.

"I look back now and I know I learned a lot of what I needed to learn in Israel. Now I'm here learning about the things you need to learn about in college, managing time and dealing with different kinds of people. When I go to theater school after I graduate, I know I'll be ready to combine the fun times with the responsibility, and study something I love."

ERIC VAN DUSEN

Marblehead, Massachusetts

UNIVERSITY OF CALIFORNIA AT BERKELEY '94

Pick any point on a map, and Eric Van Dusen will tell you how to get there. Having journeyed through Central and South America, Eric believes that in life, as in traveling, "there is always a bus to the next town."

Eric's chance to take time off materialized in a roundabout way. "I skipped the first grade, and family folklore maintained that my precociousness entitled me to take a sabbatical from school sometime in the future," he explained. "Most important, my dad was a believer in this family folklore. And he was the person in the family who made you go to school when you were sick. So if he thought it was okay, so did everyone else."

"I went to Marblehead High School in Massachusetts, and during my senior year everyone was asking me about colleges. 'Where are you going to school, Eric? Where? Where?' "

Although he was rejected by most of the colleges he applied to, Eric did manage to get into the University of California at Berkeley. But only for the second semester.

Eric's initial disappointment faded as he started planning his time off. "In retrospect, I think it was really good that I didn't get into some prestigious New England school. The change of perspective by coming out here to California and escaping Marblehead was huge."

After graduating from high school in June, Eric lived at home and worked at the local boatyard until late October. "I was pumping gas and trying to save up money so I could do something. Not being in school during the month of September was enlightening for me. I had been conditioned every year of my life to believe that summer ended on Labor Day. What a hoax. There I was, living at home and working at the local boatyard. I also got a painting job. It was incredible—September was just as nice as August. Every single person I knew was in school, and I was so psyched that I was free," he said.

Living at home, however, was not always easy for Eric. "I felt like a chump to be living at home, because I wasn't in high school anymore. Everyone was calling me from college with crazy stories, and I was just sitting at home, not doing anything. Time off gave me a brief glimpse of Existential angst: Well, what do I do if I'm not in high school and I'm not in college? What is the meaning of life?"

At the end of October, Eric left Marblehead for Guatemala. He stayed there through December, and then returned to the United States to start his first semester at Berkeley in January.

Eric gives his mom partial credit for his decision to go to Guatemala. "Our coffee table was stacked thick and sagging in the middle with publications of the East Coast liberal Establishment. It was a heavy Reagan-era period, the Contras, El Salvador. I was reading a lot about current events. My mom said, 'Why don't you talk to your aunt and uncle, they just came back from a great trip to Guatemala.' "

With the endorsement of his aunt and uncle, Eric convinced his parents to pay $600 for six weeks of language study and living with a family. "That way," said Eric, "my parents could know that I was going to study." He paid for his airfare and travel expenses.

Eric was slightly overwhelmed when he first arrived in the country. "I walked around in Guatemala City, which is this super-hellish Third World city full of really poor people. I was walking around by myself, seventeen years old, with a crew cut. I was thinking, 'This is so crazy. What am I doing here?' I had no idea what it would be like, no clue.

"The big Guatemalan oppression was in the early eighties, when they grabbed people from their homes and shot them randomly in the streets every night. By the time I was there in 1987, everything was comparatively mellow."

Eric joined what he calls the gringo influx of people who attend language school in Guatemala. He lived with an Indian family and received six hours of one-on-one language instruction each day during the week.

"Every weekend, I was doing something. It was so easy to meet people. I was in Antigua, a city in Guatemala where a lot of people are sent to learn Spanish by their NGO, their nongovernmental organization. Being seventeen was no problem; everyone thought I was twenty-five. There was always somebody young and hip and ready to go somewhere, or somebody who knew where to go and could tell me. They knew which bus to take and how to get to the rad waterfall in the jungle.

"Guatemala is such an amazing country to travel in. Packed into an area the size of Virginia, you have jungles, the Pacific Ocean, Caribbean high mountains, the indigenous culture of the Indians, all within two hours of each other."

Eric noticed many travelers whose imaginations were restricted by the guidebooks they were using. "There's this thing about people backpacking and traveling with books, like the

Lonely Planet Guides. They're useful, and I've done a lot of traveling like that. But if you use that book to get to the rad waterfall in the jungle, there will be fifteen other people there when you arrive.

"It's so much more empowering when you can go do it on your own. Show up in a town and ask, 'Where can we stay?' And you get led around in circles until you find a place. Then you can ask, 'Where can we eat?' And the town may be so small that there's only one place. So you go there."

Immersing himself in one-on-one Spanish instruction proved to be challenging for Eric. "Sitting down with someone one-on-one for six hours a day was painful sometimes, but that's **the** way to learn. My learning curve was so steep. You just have to be patient, and realize that it is unnatural to talk to someone six hours a day for five days in a row. Sometimes my instructor would look at me and say, 'You talk now.'

"There are language schools in Antigua, Quezaltenango, and now the cool place to go is Todos Santos, which is in the Indian highlands. In early 1994, it still cost only $100 a week to live with a family and do language study.

"Guatemala is a very poor country. Per capita income is much less than in the United States. Room and board, which includes three meals a day, five days a week, costs $20 a week.

"You can live with an Indian family of five people in a one-room home. And they have one extra bed where three of the kids were going to sleep. Now they're all going to sleep in the bed with the two parents and the other two kids, so that you can sleep in that bed. Other schools can hook you up with nicer accommodations, but then you may not have the same contact with the indigenous community."

Eric left Guatemala in December and came home to get ready for college. He said he was a bit confused about what to expect at Berkeley. He took a class in Latin American history during his first semester. "I totally lived for and loved that class. We studied Argentina and Chile. I also took a class on economic development. The professor made me realize that studying development and the Third World was something you could do in life. I decided to visit the countries I had been studying."

At first, Eric hoped to find a traditional study-abroad program such as Education Abroad Programs at Berkeley. "But to do EAP, you have to have taken two years of Spanish classes at Berkeley. And I'm not good at doing little homework assignments, like writing down everything with the right accent mark over and over again. Also, it's really hard to figure out from here what is up in other countries. What's the place to be? What's the good school?

"I decided to buy a one-way ticket to go from California to Chile in January of 1990. School doesn't start down there until March, so I thought I could figure out how to enroll and take classes once I arrived."

Eric discovered that there are many different ways to travel. "Sometimes in Chile I was just into the drug of traveling, into being constantly moving. I had to adjust to that more voyeuristic pace. When you see the fat American tourist pointing his video camera at the little Indian girl in the village, it's a lot weirder than seeing him point it at a cathedral in the middle of the city.

"You can be totally self-sufficient with a backpack, tent, and stove. I usually tried to find a home to stay in, and there were a lot of bed-and-breakfast-style places. You can just ask, 'Where can I stay? Do you know somebody with a room?' That way, you get to actually meet real people. You can sit in their living room and look at their pictures. They may tell you stories about their cousin living in Houston: 'Don't you know Houston? Do you know my cousin?'

"So much of people trying to learn Spanish results in a tourist saying, 'How much is this? Can I buy that?' or 'Where's the bus?' But to be able to have a conversation means being able to hear their story.

"Crime wasn't so bad in Chile. Peru was where you hear the hairy stories. People there may go at your backpack with a machete, and ten little kids will dive on your stuff while it spills out before you have a chance to grab it."

Border crossings were another occasion for heads-up behavior. Though Eric was seldom searched himself, he experienced firsthand the high drama of covert crossings from one country into another. "I was on a crowded bus driving across the border between Chile and Bolivia. The security guy came on and I was all worried about him coming to search me because I'm a gringo with long hair. And then I realized there was a forty-year-old fat señora across from me, smuggling ten thousand Snickers candy bars from the duty-free port in Chile into Bolivia. She pretended to be asleep, and when the security guy asked her what was in the bags, she said, 'Ropa, ropa, clothes, leave me alone.'"

After spending January, February, and part of March traveling in Chile and Bolivia, Eric went to Argentina. "The first day I got there, I said, 'Here I am, ta-da! I'm going to register for my classes.' The janitor was locking up the door, and he told me, 'Oh, sorry. Everyone is on strike.'

"So I head downtown, and there is a huge protest going on in the central plaza. Drums, flags, chants, and all these labor movements, including the teachers' union. I was so psyched to see a protest where labor was a real force."

School finally started two weeks later, and Eric signed up for a full load of courses. He was initially living with other Americans in a "random fucked-up hotel that I read about in a tourist guide," which wasn't helping his Spanish. "So I posted some signs that said, 'I am an American student looking for a place to share, please leave your phone number.' And people left their numbers. I ended up living with a great Argentinian guy in his twenties. I hooked up with his friends, and we would stay up late to drink, play chess, and sit around listening to tango."

Eric's style of studying abroad proved to be much cheaper than a regular program would have been. "It was so cheap because I was going to the state school and living in an apartment. It was $600 the first semester at school, and through Berkeley's EAP program it costs $3,000. And if you're willing to jump through a lot of paperwork hoops, you can get credit on your transcript," he said.

Eric strove for a more authentic experience than many people on exchange programs achieve. "The greatest thing for me was that I could just fit in and be a student. I didn't open my mouth in class for the first month. I would just go and sit there and take notes. And nobody noticed.

"I met a bunch of Americans taking classes at another university with a formal study-abroad program. They were having a good time but educationally it was a total joke. And everything was facilitated for them: 'Let's go to the meeting together. Let's have the little luncheon for all the exchange students.' Those people were still on the tour bus.

"For me to show up in Argentina, find an Argentinian to live with, go to the UBA, the University of Buenos Aires, walk in, figure out which class I wanted to go to by reading the schedule, go and sit in on a class, buy the reading from the school store, and go through the paces of a student without anyone telling me what to do—all that gave me a sense of empowerment."

After spending a semester at the UBA, Eric capped off his

trip with a 6,000-mile thirty-day overland excursion, passing through fifteen countries on his way home from Buenos Aires to Berkeley.

"I had $650, which was the cost of a one-way plane ticket home. I figured I could travel home in twelve hours with a freaky microwaved meal and a beer. Or I could have a whole month of adventures," he said.

"You can always get a bus to the next town, and you can always get a visa at the border. I was taking buses and trains, mostly buses, and hitchhiking."

Traversing the Darien Gap, which separates Colombia from Panama, was the trickiest part of Eric's journey home. "Panama was wild. From Colombia to Panama I went in a motorboat, bouncing off the Caribbean waves at six in the morning. We hit this tiny village, a random outpost of civilization. All mangoes, coconuts, and fish. Impenetrable jungle, and there were no roads.

"A Panamanian border patrolman searched me, and when he realized I was American, he walked inside and yelled, 'Hey, come out here, I've got an American for you.' Two Marines came out who were stationed in Panama following the U.S. invasion.

"One of them says to me, 'Oh, you're one of those long-haired hippie types trying to save Central America and make it safe for the Commies.' A total asshole, trying to pick a fight with me. 'No, sir,' I said. 'I'm just on my way home from the university.'

"I went to the only place around where you could eat lunch and drink a beer. While I was there, this huge military helicopter lands and out steps the colonel. He is walking down the main street and looks over at me. And there I am, sitting in my chair drinking a beer. I have on a T-shirt with Edward

Munch's painting *The Scream*, of a guy with no ears standing on a bridge and filling the whole canvas with his anguished howl. My T-shirt was captioned 'President Quayle.'

" 'Who's that?' asks the colonel.

" 'Uh, I don't know, sir. He's a visiting traveling student, sir.'

"So the colonel comes over to say hello and ask me if I'm enjoying my stay. He's talking to me as if this situation is totally normal. So I ask him, 'Please, sir, might I have a ride across the Darien Gap with you? Please, can I go on the chopper? Because the only way for me to get out of here is to hike through the jungle for a week.'

" 'Not with that shirt you won't,' the colonel told me.

"So I took the mail plane that comes through once a week. We flew over a huge coral archipelago, landing on these tiny islands. Water, airstrip, water—it's totally hairy. And there is a guy sitting in a hammock by the runway. Turns out he's the mailman. He gets up, saunters over. The pilot gives him two letters and he gives him one letter, and we get back in the plane.

"We stopped at one settlement where Indians came up in huge dugout canoes, with big necklaces, totally dressed up, and put one of their guys on the plane next to me. He's never been on a plane before, so he's petrified. And we take off as they're canoeing away, waving up to us. Half an hour later, we were in Panama City.

"The way I made it across from South to Central America was not in any book at all. I just did it by going to the next town. There's always a way to go to the next town," he said.

Eric has since graduated from Berkeley and is pursuing a Ph.D. in agricultural economics at the University of California at Davis. His studies there have given him a chance to continue traveling in the developing world as part of his research.

"I definitely recommend taking time off. Get as far off your beaten track you can. For some people, going to Europe can be a truly amazing experience. For others, it's Eurail hell. 'Oh, and then we went to Amsterdam and smoked hash. And then we went to Munich and drank beer. And then we went to Prague and tripped out. Prague was so romantic. And then we went to Italy and saw the *David*.' So many Americans do that.

"The message I would want to put out is how much it meant to me just to do it on my own. The hardest part is leaving the United States and getting the money together. You might have supportive parents, but you might not be able to say, 'Dad, I need some money. I'm going to Argentina by myself, and I'm going to learn more than I would if I went through a university.' Parents are used to writing checks to institutions, not ideas.

"There's nothing like being in a tiny Honduran town, eating pineapple and watching the chickens fight. Or if you're in a rain forest, and it hits you that nature is a total miracle. The parrots and tarantulas aren't there for me to see them; they're just there.

"How can you communicate that to somebody? All you can say is, it's worth it. It will be that good if you do it. Just give yourself enough credit to try."

PART THREE

Community Service and Volunteer Work

Students who wish to take time off to volunteer for a particular cause or organization can do so in a number of ways. Some organizations provide volunteers with room, board, and a small stipend. Many unpaid volunteers view the experience they gain as their wages. If you want to work for an organization that does not have a funded position available for you, you will have to come up with the money on your own. You may be able to do so by splitting your time off in half. Many students live at home for six months to work and save money and then volunteer in the second half of their year off. Others find a part-time job to go with a part-time volunteer position.

Volunteering in the United States

CORY MASON

Racine, Wisconsin
CENTENARY COLLEGE '97

While Cory Mason's friends were busily filling out college applications, he was on the way to setting a record for skipping the most days of school and still graduating.

Cory had begun high school full of enthusiasm, lettering on the varsity swim team as a freshman and eventually qualifying for swim nationals. "Any self-discipline I've ever had comes from swimming," Cory observed. "Practice is grueling: you go back and forth over and over again. There's no change of scenery, and you can't really talk to anybody."

Cory attended a public high school in Racine, Wisconsin, with 2,400 students. He was in the international baccalaureate program, which he described as "almost a school within a school." IB programs usually consist of an accelerated work-intensive course of study for talented students, and they can be found in many countries. "Out of six hundred kids in my graduating class," Cory said, "fifty were in the IB program. We had the best teachers in each department, which was an unfair advantage, but we had a lot more homework, too."

Early on in high school, many of Cory's friends came from swimming. "There were three or four of us who got on the varsity level freshman year. That was great, but they hazed the hell out of us. One time they tied up one of my friends naked in a towel bag, threw him into the pool during girls' swim class, and when he got out of the bag, there he was, stark naked. It was awful."

Because of the swim meets he participated in every weekend, the Mason family could no longer go to church on Sundays. "Sometimes we'd go fifteen weekends in a row where we'd be at swim meets every weekend. It consumed our entire life. My dad looked at that time the family spent together as our church. He firmly believed that religion didn't necessarily have to take place in church, and he was glad that his family was together and that his kids were doing something constructive."

Swimming started to wear on Cory at the end of high school, and a shoulder injury increased his ambivalence about the sport. "It dawned on me, was it really worth it to work hard seven months at a crack, without a break, in order to drop my time by half a second?

"I went through a period where I just felt real blasé about everything. It drove my parents up the wall. Some people at my school went through a senior slump; I had a senior plummet. The last two years of high school seemed to last forever. I wanted to be grownup and have real responsibilities."

Like all his friends, Cory went through the motions of applying to colleges during his senior year. As the time approached to make a decision, however, he became certain that going straight to college was not for him. "It just seemed that everybody I knew was going to the University of Wisconsin at Madison. A lot of kids from my school go there and only hang out with the kids they knew from high school. That just seems so limiting, and I was really scared that was going to happen to me."

In the midst of a difficult senior year, Cory also was going through a year-long confirmation program with his priest, Father Bruce. "Father Bruce was really cool; he's the only priest I know who wears an earring. The main group met on Sunday nights and we had a smaller group that met on Tuesday nights to discuss things in greater depth.

"Our small group studied the vow of nonviolence, not just physical violence, but also violence of the heart and mind. We are in a society that is constantly bombarded with violence. Our entire legal system is adversarial; our political system is confrontational. I was learning more through confirmation than I was in school."

Cory's confirmation program also included community service. "During Christmas, we were each given a family that we had to raise money for. We organized a Polar Bear plunge. We ran into Lake Michigan on January 14. The water was freezing, and they had an ambulance on hand. A couple of us were crazy enough to swim out to the buoy and back. We got on the front page of the newspaper. It's now become a tradition, and we bring in a couple thousand dollars every year."

Cory recalls telling Father Bruce that he was not ready to go to college. "I had heard so many stories about the kids at Madison. They go up there, party all the time, don't go to class, and flunk out their first semester. What a waste. And I tell you, that would have been me."

When Cory asked Father Bruce if he knew anything about missionary work, Father Bruce gave him some booklets. Unfortunately, many of the organizations only wanted people who were at least twenty-one years old. "You would think, with something like missionary work, that when someone asks to volunteer they'd do everything they could to encourage that person and help him or her set it up. It was the most bureaucratic thing I've ever been involved with."

Cory's parents wondered what he was doing. "I had to explain to them why we had this astronomical phone bill, including calls to Venezuela. I told them I was thinking about taking time off and investigating the possibilities of some kind of religiously inspired community service in South America. My dad said, 'Cory, I know so many kids that took time off and never came back. It's rough out there in the real world.' I said, 'Yeah, yeah, you're right,' but with my mom, who knew I was not ready for college, I convinced him to give me the benefit of the doubt."

Cory applied to work for Habitat for Humanity and was accepted in June. Habitat for Humanity is an organization dedicated to providing affordable housing for low-income families. Habitat now has affiliates in forty-five countries, with close to 1,200 chapters in the United States.

Habitat gave Cory a choice of three sites: Ontario, Canada; Waco, Texas; and Savannah, Georgia. "I decided on Savannah because they let me be project manager, and the fact that it was ten miles away from the ocean was real appealing. The town is beautiful, right on the Savannah River."

Cory's duties as project manager included helping build houses, overseeing and managing the construction sites, and training the volunteers and recipient families. In return for his services, he was given room, board, and a stipend of $20 a week. "It was rough getting by on $20 a week," he said. "And if you wanted to use the truck, you had to put gas in it. It was an old beat-up Chevy truck that gets something like eight miles to the gallon, and you had to drive all the way into town and all the way back."

Cory was in charge of a project to build fifty-two new houses on a thirteen-acre site in rural Savannah. "I had never built a house before, nor had I lifted a hammer to do anything aside from hang a picture on a wall." But Cory caught on quickly. He figured out a lot on his own, and he also had two teachers—the other project manager at his site, and a construction superintendent hired by Habitat.

Habitat builds houses which vary in size, depending on the size of the recipient family, with an average of 1,500 square feet per home. The houses come with heat and central air, a stove, and a refrigerator. Habitat sells the houses for approximately $30,000, an affordable price achieved through private donations of money, labor, and materials.

Recipient families chosen by a Habitat committee are required to put five hundred hours of "sweat equity" into the house. They then buy the house with a no-interest mortgage which can be paid back over the course of fifteen to twenty-five years.

"Working for Habitat was a real eye-opening experience," Cory explained. "There are families in America who are living in Third World conditions. Unfortunately, charity is usually directed to the so-called deserving poor in our country, those people who have jobs and are trying to make a go of it. Meanwhile, we call the poor people most in need of assistance 'undeserving' and ignore them.

"I heard a social worker give a speech in Savannah called 'Standing Next to Pain,' and he said that it was important to try and walk in other people's shoes. He said, 'Look, everybody's got pain, but in addition to the pain of being alive, which we all share—becoming sick and losing loved ones—the poor are stricken with the pain of poverty.' "

Cory found it inspiring to work with people from varied backgrounds. "The thing about working construction is, nobody wears nice clothes. People would show up in jeans and T-shirts. Most of the rich people who volunteered from the nearby retirement community didn't know much about construction, and neither did most of the recipients. That was one of the neatest things about working there; seeing people from all different walks of life coming together and deciding they were going to put up a wall that afternoon."

The most difficult part of Cory's stay in Savannah came toward the end of February. "Habitat International had what's called the Spring Break Challenge. They go to college campuses and recruit groups to work at a site for a week. I was a little worried about telling these twenty-two-year-olds what to do. I thought they were going to say, 'You're just a little punk out of high school. What are you talking about?' But when it came right down to it, most of them had no clue about construction, and I did."

"We went forty-three days straight without a day off. It was rough, because at night in the dormitories they'd say, 'We want to see what Savannah's like, can you show us around the town?' By the time I left, I could have applied to be a tour guide for the summer."

When Cory left Savannah, he was able to get a job working construction in Racine. "It was great, because I was learning a trade. I learned all about roofing, Sheetrock, electricity, and a little bit about plumbing."

After working in Racine for the summer, Cory enrolled at Centenary College, a small Methodist-affiliated liberal-arts school in Shreveport, Louisiana.

"Coming back to Racine was good. I had been at odds with my parents when I was living at home my senior year. When I came back, they were actually glad to have me. Earlier, my dad had been kind of worried. His oldest son, who was supposed to go off to college, was doing something kind of wacky. But by the time I left for Centenary, he was actually proud of what I had done and would tell people at work about it.

"For a long time, I took great pride in being discontent with everything around me. There was a certain appeal to that, being a pain in the ass. That's not to say that I don't still question things that go on around me. The biggest change, though, is that now I'm at peace with myself.

"I see kids in college who could be learning a lot more by just taking a year off and working somewhere. You learn to pay your bills. You have to make sure you know where your next meal is coming from. You also learn that if you don't have an education you can't get a stable job. I didn't like scraping by on $20 a week, and I don't want to scrape for my next meal the rest of my life.

"You can't learn that without leaving school. In college, you just live in your dorm room, all your meals are cooked for you, and it's pretty simple. All you have to do is show up."

BRENDAN ROBINSON

Boston, Massachusetts

JOHNSON C. SMITH COLLEGE '98

For Brendan Robinson, *Boyz 'N the Hood* was not just a movie. It was his life. "Most of my friends came from Cathedral Projects, a housing project in the South End section of Boston. In the beginning, we were little shorties, little kids doing little-kid things like riding bikes together," he said.

When he was twelve, Brendan and his friends formed a gang. "We started a group, the little Heath Streets. We were into breakdancing and pretending to be rappers. Then it grew into something I'm not proud to say I was part of. When you gangbang, you have to do a certain amount of criminal activity, called dirt. Once you reach a certain point, you're not a little kid anymore. You're what you call a G, a Gangster, or an OG, an Original Gangster."

Belonging to a gang gave Brendan a tremendous sensation of power. "Gangbanging takes you way beyond acceptance, way beyond love, way beyond colors. It was energy. I could go to a party and if anyone tried to kick my ass, they would have twenty other guys to deal with. And if it really got ridiculous, I could get on the phone and have everybody down there."

Things began to fall apart when crack and guns hit the neighborhood at the same time. "One day they weren't there and the next day they were. Not too many people knew it would be a multibillion-dollar business," he said.

A steady and diverse stream of customers came to Brendan in search of crack. "I'd get white guys with a suit and tie on, driving up in a Lexus, risking their lives driving through the projects just so they can get their high.

"Those are the people that would be home reading a newspaper or watching the evening news about the inner city, and say, 'Damn, honey, do you believe what those people are doing!' Just a couple hours earlier, they were doing exactly what they were describing on the news, buying drugs."

When Brendan bumped into his white customers in other parts of the city, most of them ignored him. "Those are the same people who won't give you a job. I've had white people say, 'Hey, buddy, how are you?' when they wanted drugs. On the train, they just turned their head away from me. I thought, 'Next time I see you down in the projects, I'm not going to recognize you and we'll see how it feels. Probably lonesome and scary.' "

The deaths of people close to him began to take a toll on Brendan's psyche. "I spent a lot of time talking with my best friend, Randy, about how we wished we were never in this life to begin with.

"I remember waiting for the bus to go to school one day during the spring of my freshman year. It was 6:30 a.m. on March 21. Randy walked by and said, 'Yo, B., why don't you hook school with me and chill with these girls I'm going to go meet now?' He wasn't a school-going kind of guy."

Brendan told Randy he would catch up with him after school and they gave each other a parting hug. "Then a car pulled around that had already passed by a few times. There was a kid in there that Randy had shot at a party two months earlier during a fight over a girl. He had a big gauze bandage on his neck.

"I heard four gunshots. I started running down the street and I knew it was Randy. It felt like someone had stuck a pin in my heart and all my feelings went numb."

As he sprinted toward Randy, Brendan ran into the person with the gauze patch on his neck. "When he saw me coming, he took his gun out and pointed it at me. When he pulled back the handle, there were no bullets left.

"I wasn't thinking at the time about how close I came to dying. I was thinking about Randy. He was peeled over a porch in a prone position with blood everywhere. He looked really cold and was shaking a lot."

Brendan held Randy in his arms until the paramedics arrived. "Before they put him in the ambulance, the last thing he said to me was 'I love you.' His parents were dead. I was the only person left in the world who cared about him. Randy was DOA at the hospital," he said.

Brendan started to think about doing things differently. "I remember sitting in the dark for hours and crying. When I reflected on my life, I wasn't too pleased with myself. I was having a lot of nightmares and cold sweats."

When a government-sponsored program offered Brendan a place in a white high school in the suburbs of Boston, he took it. "To join some gangs, you have to kill someone. And if you leave, you will be murdered. My gang was a little different. People knew me, and knew that I was serious about my education. I always loved going to school. My OGs would always point me out and say, 'He's going to make it.' They wanted me to go to school and better myself.

"My mother always told me 'You're better than that' when we saw hoodlums on our street. I just stayed away from Boston as much as possible. After a while, it worked. I wasn't a part of Heath anymore."

During his final year of high school in 1993, Brendan's mother urged him to look into City Year. City Year brings together young people from diverse racial, ethnic, and socio-economic backgrounds for a demanding year of full-time community service and leadership development. The corps members, ages seventeen to twenty-three, include college graduates, high school graduates, and people without high school diplomas.

Alan Khazei and Michael Brown, roommates at Harvard Law School, founded City Year in 1988 as a fifty-person summer pilot program in Boston. Cited by President Clinton as the model for his national service legislation, City Year has expanded to include over six hundred corps members in Chicago, Illinois; San Jose, California; Providence, Rhode Island; Columbus, Ohio; San Antonio, Texas; and Columbia, South Carolina.

Brendan sent in his application and was called in to City Year for an interview. "I go down there and these were the most happy-go-lucky people I'd ever seen. They were really excited about what they were doing, and they were happy to see me."

Brendan was struck by the diversity of City Year, some of which made him uncomfortable. "You would have ex-gangbangers working side by side with rich white college kids. I remember thinking, 'I'm not going to work with any faggots.'"

City Year corps members participate in a wide variety of

service activities. Typical projects might give corps members a chance to serve as teachers' aides in public schools, renovate low-income housing, or volunteer in homeless shelters. "I remember thinking, 'You know what, I have a chance to give back something positive. Maybe I won't have nightmares anymore.' "

In return for a year of hard work, corps members receive a stipend of $125 a week, are awarded $5,000 for higher education or job training upon completion of the program, and have access to college and career counseling services.

In addition to weekly leadership and community building workshops, City Year requires corps members who have not graduated from high school to take high school equivalency classes. If they keep up with the work, corps members can earn their GED.

"We had to sign a contract that explained what was expected of us in terms of attendance, punctuality, and behavior. If you don't stick to the contract, you're out of the program. I had to be smart, sharp, and prompt at all times."

Brendan thought City Year's expectations were reasonable. "In the contract, it said, 'Be here at 8:15 a.m.' I don't care if you have been abused all your life, you can make it here at 8:15.

"We worked every day, Monday through Friday, 8:15 a.m. to 6 p.m., from September to June. We began each morning with PT, physical training. After the half hour of calisthenics, we fanned out in teams of ten to different project sites around the city."

The city of Boston supplied corps members with free subway passes as a demonstration of support. "You would always see City Year kids on the T, Boston's subway. It was easy to spot us—bright red jackets, black City Year sweatshirts, khaki pants, and Timberland boots," he said.

Brendan knew the program was going to be hard for him, so he made himself a promise on the first day. "I told myself that whatever was to happen, as far as I was to go, or as low as I was to go, no matter how hard it got, I was not going to quit."

Somewhat unexpectedly, Brendan found himself in charge of teaching photography in an after-school program for kids who lived in a housing project near Cambridge. "My team leader said, 'Okay, who likes photography?' I raised my hand and said, 'I've taken a few pictures.' He said, 'Great. You're the new photography teacher.' Some City Year people taught me everything they knew, and I read some books to learn more."

To sign up kids for his class, Brendan did an outreach program in the neighborhood. "I went out and got the kids most people wouldn't even think of talking to. The ones drinking the 40s and smoking the weed at thirteen by the basketball courts."

Brendan convinced eighteen kids to sign up for his class. "I gave them different assignments and told them they were not allowed to come back unless they'd done their homework. I told them, 'If you are going to take a picture of something, have a story to tell with it. And if you don't have a story, make one up.' That was my way of opening their minds. Then I would have them write up the story as a way of teaching them spelling and English."

In addition to the regular workday, Brendan also threw himself into extracurricular activities at City Year. His fellow corps members elected Brendan to lead the Corps Action Council, a liaison group between corps members and administrators at City Year. "I gave speeches at meetings and people liked them. I would speak about urban violence, drugs, gangs,

AIDS [Brendan's father had recently died of AIDS], and inter-racial relationships. Things that had affected my life."

When some of Brendan's speeches brought hundreds of cheering and crying people to their feet, higher-ups at City Year started giving Brendan even greater responsibilities and opportunities. "Michael Brown, the co-founder, took me with him on a trip to meet with senators in Washington, D.C. I discussed my life history and experience with City Year in a meeting where we asked for more support for the program. I shook hands with President Clinton.

"Best of all, City Year was planning to open a new site in Chicago and I was chosen to be on the expansion team that moved there. They sent the Chicago expansion team on a training retreat. My bags were packed and I was all ready to move to a new city."

Brendan never made it to Chicago. "On the very last day of training, I was playing basketball with some corps members. One guy, an ex-crack addict from South Boston, started talking shit to me. Then all of a sudden he took a basketball and threw it at my head."

Brendan's assailant came at him swinging and a fight broke out. "He found himself on the ground right quick with my foot going down his throat. Unfortunately, Michael and Alan were right there watching. They yanked me from the expansion team."

Alan Khazei agreed to meet with Brendan to discuss the incident. "I wanted a second chance. I told him, 'Dude, if someone came at you swinging, I'm sure you would defend yourself.' He said, 'No, I'd get punched in the face.' I said, 'Alan, as far as I'm concerned, if you came at me swinging, I'd knock you out, too. I don't know too many people who don't defend themselves and their family.'

"I knew that I was not God's gift to City Year, but I had really tried my best. That was the closest I came to quitting City Year, when Alan Khazei told me he would have taken those punches. I had done outreach programs at high schools for City Year and preached about City Year's diversity, open-mindedness, and commitment to giving people a second chance. I felt betrayed. Here's my top guy basically telling me 'Fuck you.' I almost felt like getting up and punching him to see what he really would have done."

Brendan decided to stick to his original promise and finished out his time with City Year. The mother of a fellow corps member had heard about Brendan and offered to help him get into college. "She said, 'Meet with me, and if you impress me, I will write a letter of recommendation on your behalf.' With her help, I got in," he said.

Brendan was accepted at Johnson C. Smith University in Charlotte, North Carolina, for the 1994–95 school year. "I had never heard of the school, had never been down to the South, didn't know anything about Charlotte, and was very skeptical about going," he said.

Successfully completing City Year entitled Brendan to $5,000, money which helped convince him to give college a try. Going from the diversity of City Year to an all-black college was difficult. "There was some hatred toward whites on campus that was hard for me to deal with." Having a white mother and a black father sometimes made life complicated for Brendan. "Being a mulatto was hard. Lots of Oreo cookie jokes," he said.

Brendan's favorite class was one where he read *Jonathan Livingston Seagull*, by Richard Bach. The book is about a seagull whose love for flying isolates him from his fellow birds. "I told the people in the class that I felt like an outsider because I couldn't agree with what they were saying about white people.

When they said, 'All white people do this,' I said, 'You're wrong. My mother is white and she doesn't do that. My mother gave up her life to raise me and my brother.' "

Brendan plans to finish college and then pursue a master's degree in social work. "I want to spend my life reaching back, helping other people in situations like mine to get out.

"There needs to be a change. There are 27,000 golf courses in America and we still have people living in the streets who can't feed themselves."

Would he recommend City Year to other people? "City Year has problems just like any other organization. They're not perfect, but they're trying. Is City Year right for you? I don't know you. You better look into it yourself."

Brendan said the most important thing he learned was to accept people for who they are. "I met the first gay person I'd ever respected. It opened my mind to the fact that gays are just like everyone else. They should not be treated like faggots, because they're not faggots. That's like calling a black person a nigger. They're not a nigger, they're a human being."

AKIIMA PRICE

Temple Hills, Maryland

UNIVERSITY OF MARYLAND EASTERN SHORE '96

Akiima Price was seven years old when she realized that her mother was white.

"I didn't figure it out until my mom dropped me off at school one day and my friends looked at her and said, 'Who's that?' I got this vibe that something was wrong, and I said, 'Oh, she's just the neighbor.' When you're black and your mother is white, your life is going to be a little bit different.

"To me she was just my mom, and the story was never a big deal. In sixth grade, I wrote a personal essay about my family for a writing assignment. The teacher left the room with it, and she came back with some other teachers who were all crying. They said to me, 'Akiima, this is beautiful. You have to continue to write.' "

At about the same time, Akiima developed a passion for radio, taking every opportunity to read the lunch menu or the bus schedule over the loudspeaker at school. In the meantime, she took her teachers' advice and began keeping a diary.

"I grew up with really low self-esteem. I had a lot of problems with my stepmother, so I really feared being at home, and I was heavy as a child, so I was cast aside for that. So I cried a lot and I wrote a lot. That's when I really began to develop my writing."

In high school, her first serious boyfriend put her in touch with religion. "I started going to church with him, and I understood who God was and what he had for me, and I said, 'You know what, there **is** going to be a life for me.' "

She wanted to go on to college, but her father discouraged her from going right away. "My father told me to take a year off to figure out what I wanted to do. It hurt. I told him that all my friends were going to college, but he said that money was tight."

Akiima read the want ads and found a job as a receptionist. Her employer moved her to data entry but later decided to let her go. She bounced right back and found a job as a day-care assistant for the remainder of her year off.

In the fall of 1991, Akiima started college. She chose to attend the University of Maryland Eastern Shore, a historically black college of 2,500 undergraduates.

During her freshman year, Akiima took an environmental science class. "A woman named Raquel Jones came to my class and showed slides of kids working in the environment. She said, 'How would you like to make money and go places?' I said, 'Well, that sounds good.' "

Raquel was there to pitch the Student Conservation Association, an organization which pays hundreds of students to work in national parks and forests all over the country each year.

"I figured I wasn't going to get accepted because it didn't have anything to do with my major. But they had a special program trying to get minorities interested in conservation work. Something inside me said to just try it, and I was accepted," she said.

Akiima's group of SCA interns attended an orientation session in Virginia in the beginning of the summer of 1992. "They train you in whatever ways they can—networking, résumé writing, and issues in conservation. Then they send you off."

Akiima was assigned to the Lake Mead National Recreation Area, thirty miles from Las Vegas. "I got there and I was thinking, 'Oh God, what am I doing here?' It was nighttime, and it was about 104 degrees. My big thing was spiders. I had really bad arachnophobia, and there were all these spiders and bugs in the house where I was living. One of the first nights there, I saw a big bug. I had to sleep sitting up in a chair in the living room."

Despite being left speechless with fear by the spiders, at work Akiima was able to put her communications skills to use soon after arriving. "I was working with kids and other visitors at Lake Mead, and I'm a people person, so I was able to find my release there. When I first got there, I worked at the visitors' center answering questions. Then they had an environmental education program where kids came to learn more about the desert.

"Right off the bat, I started telling the rangers what they were doing wrong. I was sure they were going to ask me to leave, but instead they said, 'No, that's great, tell us more. So I started developing new educational programs, creative ways to teach the kids."

The rangers were so impressed with Akiima's work that they invited her back the following summer. When her second summer at Lake Mead ended, they asked that she stay for the entire semester and apply for grant money to continue her programs, and she agreed.

"They wanted me to continue to work on programs to get inner-city kids to respect the land and be interested in the parks. And I said, 'Excuse me, but how are you going to get them to respect the land when they don't even respect themselves?'

"So I wrote up a program called the Keys program. We all come to doors that we can't unlock alone. People assume that if one notch is off and they can't unlock the door, they should just throw away the key. They assume the whole key is bad. Well, when these kids come in, they're blank keys. You can teach them self-esteem, teach them about their heritage," Akiima explained.

SCA interns are paid $3,500 for the summer and also receive $100 every two weeks for food. "That paid my tuition," Akiima noted. Interns live for free in park housing. During her semester off, Akiima was promoted to junior ranger, and she earned $7.50 an hour. "It was great. That money was direct-deposited into my account, so I was experiencing all these adult-like things."

Every day, Akiima arrived at work at 7:30 a.m. and worked until at least four. "At the end, there was nothing to come home to. We had no television and no radio, because we were in the middle of mountains. Even when I turned twenty-one, all there was to do if you didn't have much money was go to the country bars in Las Vegas. Most of the time, I came home and thought about what I wanted to do in my life and how I was going to get there.

"My first year back in school was great. Everything I learned in SCA, from hiking to networking, has taken some part of my life to where I needed it to go. At first, I didn't know what I would use the skills for. But it's like someone has given you all these coins, and they don't work as money, so you don't know what to do with them. Then you come to these tolls, and you say, 'Wow! I can pay with these.'"

Akiima's only problem with reentering school was her feeling that her friends had not changed or grown at the same rate she had. "I was moving, and they were standing still. I'm not saying that moving at one time or another is better. Some of them tried to walk with me, but they couldn't really understand. They were like, 'Yeah, I'm proud of you, but I can't relate.' "

Her professors, however, noticed the difference immediately. "My relationship with my teachers was much better."

In the summer of 1993, Akiima returned to Lake Mead to see the legacy she had left there. "They take bits and pieces from my Keys program now. They're white and the kids who come are black. If you're on different sides of a lake, and one group has food while the other is hungry, just because you build a bridge doesn't mean that the hungry group will be fed.

"At Lake Mead, one group has what the other one needs. The kids provide the lake with the diversity that they want to have there, and the rangers can provide kids with an opportunity to learn and better themselves. I just served as the ambassador.

"It kind of threw me off, sitting at graduation in 1995, because I could have been walking if I hadn't taken that semester off to work for SCA," Akiima said. "But I look back, and I think, 'Would I have walked proud, as I'm going to walk at graduation? Would I have walked strong? Would my grades be the same? Would I have been as focused? No.' "

Nor would she have the pet tarantula that lives in her room now. "Oh, yeah," she said. "I kicked the arachnophobia my second summer there."

GIEV KASHKOOLI

Palo Alto, California

BROWN UNIVERSITY '94

During his sophomore year at Brown University, Giev Kashkooli started to question the connections between what he was studying in the classroom and what he was learning outside it.

He was volunteering with abused and homeless children in Providence, and one boy in particular made him think. "I had a kid ask me once, 'What are you doing here? Are you being paid a lot of money?' I laughed and said, 'I'm here because people like you are teaching me stuff.' "

When Giev asked himself what he was doing at Brown, he didn't know the answer. "I realized I had no idea what my liberal arts education was preparing me for. I didn't even know if it was useful. I wanted to do something that would help me decide what else I needed to learn while I was at Brown.

"I had a confrontation one time with some of the people I was doing the community service with. I was teaching the kids what I had learned about education: the most important thing is that you are curious and challenge authority. More important than what you were studying was how you were studying it.

"People told me that was a bad approach, that I was teaching these abused and homeless kids a rich person's education. I needed to know more about the world outside of school. If I'm teaching these kids only what I've known, and I don't really know that much . . ."

Giev started to formulate a plan for his time off that would provide him with an opportunity to learn Spanish, the first language of many of the children he had been working with. "I knew I wanted to live in a city. And I knew I wanted a job that would make me self-sufficient financially. I also hoped the job would let me save enough money to fund the second half of the year, when I wanted to travel and learn Spanish."

Giev began his job search early on—"I thought it was one of those things you were supposed to do"—but discovered many places did not hire far in advance. "Besides learning how to write a résumé and cover letter, which I had never done before, I learned general things about searching for a job that were invaluable when I graduated."

Giev had to change his plans slightly when he looked into the cost of living in a major city and learned the salaries offered by most public-service organizations. "I couldn't get a job and live in a city and have it finance the second half of my year. So I realized that I was going to have to return home to California and get a summer job that was going to pay me a fair amount of money.

"My younger brother also needed a job. So we decided we would go to all these real estate agents throughout the Bay Area. When you're trying to sell a house, the agent is always trying to get the owners to fix it up. And the owner never wants to fix it up and mow the lawn, because it costs too much money. Sometimes the agents would pay us themselves. I earned $10 an hour for being a handyman, mostly just general gardening and painting. We made up flyers and did the whole thing ourselves. I made a ton of money that summer."

Meanwhile, Giev's search for a job for the fall was proceeding in a somewhat erratic fashion. "By May, I had three job interviews set up. I was thinking, 'This is great, I have this thing taken care of. And then I'll go to Central America.' Then all of a sudden they all fell through. When I went to interview for a job in Boston, they said, 'Actually, we don't have a job available.' I was shocked."

Giev turned to other strategies. "Tell everyone you can that you're planning on taking time off. Tell them what you're doing, because you find things in random places.

"A friend told me he had been at Stanford University's career counseling office and seen a couple of jobs that might interest me. I found a job listing to work with the Neighborhood Defender Service of Harlem as a college intern for about $250 per week. I thought I had hit the lottery. Then I kept reading and came upon the application's due date: July 12. And it was July 13.

"That's another big suggestion. If you really want something, go for it. I called them up and said, 'Look, I really want this job, and I'm perfect for it.' They agreed to send me an application and said they had not yet completed their hiring process."

Giev sent in his application and called NDS each week after that, but they took their time making a decision. "Labor Day weekend rolls around, and I decide to go camping for a few days. So I drive over to my girlfriend Catherine's house and she's shouting at me: 'Giev, your mother's on the phone. NDS just called.'

"They said they still hadn't decided yet. The next thing I remember was, I called them from wherever we were camping.

They said, 'Yes, you're hired, but you have to be here on Tuesday.' "

A few days later, Giev flew to New York City and began looking for an apartment.

"I found an apartment within a week. College campuses are really good resources—that's how I found my job and that's how I came up with a place to live. I arrived in September when all the students were looking for housing and roommates. There were flyers everywhere.

"On Tuesday, I started work at NDS, which is in the heart of Harlem. The next weekend, I looked at ten apartments. One guy wanted to rent me his walk-in closet for $400 a month. Finally, I bargained a guy down from $550 to $500 a month. It was near work, so my rationalization was that I would save $60 a month because I would be the only person in New York who actually walked to work."

Giev finally found out why NDS had been so reluctant to give him a definite answer. "Basically, they told me if I hadn't kept on calling there's no way they would have hired me. They wanted to hire someone from New York. They wanted interns from Harlem and the South Bronx, since those are the communities they serve."

NDS combines social and legal services in one community-based public defender's program. They try to find nonprison sentencing alternatives for people who normally wouldn't be able to afford a lawyer. "My job was to find out what the alternatives were and to present them to the attorney handling the case. I learned how to read a rap sheet, a person's criminal record, investigate a crime scene, and read a police report.

"If you don't have bail money in New York City, you can sit in jail for months before anything really happens. Things get backed up in a big city. Our goal was to be known in the community. That way, if someone got arrested, we could be at the police precinct that night. The person who gets arrested calls Grandma, Grandma calls us, and we go with Grandma.

"First, I would try to get as much information as possible from the person who was accused of the crime. Then I would try to get as much information as possible from the victims of the crime. I would tell them who I was and they'd say, 'Wait a minute, you're representing the motherfucker who . . .' I'd say, 'Well, we're representing the person who is **accused** of that.' "

One of Giev's most challenging assignments was to mentor an eighteen-year-old as part of an alternative sentencing deal. "An NDS attorney I was working with came to me and said, 'Look, Giev, there's this eighteen-year-old, and I want you to be like his big brother. I want you doing everything with this guy, to keep him out of trouble.'

"I knew right away that was not the best idea. He was one of eighteen children and had a huge rap sheet, mostly for stealing subway tokens to support his crack habit. The last thing a kid with seventeen brothers and sisters needs is another brother.

"So I met with him and asked him, 'What's the deal? What's going on here?' I wanted to know why he had agreed to work with me. His motivation was that he didn't want to be in prison, which I had no problem with. I wouldn't want to be in prison either. The judge told him, 'Okay, I won't put you in prison now, but if you come back here, you're in for two years, not one.' So he took a big-time gamble.

"We were supposed to get him back in school, into a job-training program, and into drug treatment. Turns out he had dropped out of school in seventh grade and hadn't learned anything before or since. He was just worried about getting something to eat. He had been homeless twice. I went to hang out at his place, it was a three-bedroom apartment for fifteen people. There was no electricity. They were heating the place with the oven on full-blast. He was definitely taking me places I'd never been before.

"He knew that I couldn't understand his world, and I never pretended to. The kind of stress that this kid was under, facing two years of prison and a drug habit that was kicking his butt, facing the fact that two of his brothers had been killed and that he had no idea who his father was. If he looked at what his life possibilities were, where he was and how far he would have to go . . . We pulled some strings here and there, I worked my ass off, but he ended up going to prison in the end."

Following a budget was crucial for Giev to make ends meet in New York. "I made sure I brought my lunch to work every day. I spent $35 a week on food. I also planned for my phone bill each month. And I did a lot of walking around the city during my free time."

Luckily, he lost his money only once. "New York is hyped up as a really dangerous place. The biggest thing I learned was that people don't trust you. When I told a friend I'd lost my wallet to a guy who said he had a knife, he told me, 'That's not mugging. That's aggressive panhandling.' "

Giev's job at NDS ended in January and he left for Guatemala a few weeks later. "NDS had many Spanish-speaking clients, so they had a Spanish teacher come in once a week, which helped me get ready for Central America.

"I went to a language school in Guatemala that also taught you about the politics of the country, but I had made a conscious decision not to actually get involved politically. I was going there to learn Spanish. My political activism could come when I was back in the States.

"You should make a reservation unless you're willing to be down there not learning Spanish while you wait. You should also find out what's going on ahead of time. Talk to as many people as possible. It's good to know things like 'Oh, yeah, soldiers with machine guns often pull you off buses in the middle of the night and search you. And that's no big deal.'

"The first two weeks were exciting but exhausting. I was dreaming verb conjugations. It was an amazing personal experience to communicate with an incredibly limited vocabulary. All I could say was things like 'Hi, my name is Giev. I eat chicken. I like lunch. I brushed my teeth this morning.' If that's all you know, that's all you can talk about," he said.

After three months in Guatemala, Giev traveled to Costa Rica in search of a job that would provide him with room and board in exchange for work. "I found out that it's good to travel with at least two letters of recommendation. When I was applying for jobs in Costa Rica, they wanted letters from institutions in the United States saying, 'In all the time I've known Giev, he has been responsible.' You can find out information like that by calling the country's embassy in America."

Other good information came from fellow travelers, one of whom told Giev about a job opening. "I landed a beauty of a job working in a national park. It was on the coast and extended back into a rain forest. My duties included greeting tourists, digging holes for toilets, cleaning up the beach, and doing trail maintenance. It was unbelievable.

"For the last few weeks, I was stationed by myself. My only job was to make sure nobody was trespassing in the area. There I am, sitting by the ocean, with my whole year behind me. It gave me a great chance to reflect on my time off and think about what I wanted to do when I came back."

Giev came home to Palo Alto, California, and worked as a painter and carpenter to save up money for school. The summer before he graduated, Giev worked with the United Farm

Workers in California. He then wrote his senior thesis about the organization's history and the impact of agricultural legislation on migrant farm workers.

"I realized that a liberal arts education is a good thing. It **is** important that you know how to write well, speak clearly, and think critically. I had to prepare documents for judges with somebody's life on the line."

SUSAN STEELE

Woodstock, Vermont

UNIVERSITY OF VERMONT '95

Susan Steele knew it was possible to take time off after finishing high school in Woodstock, Vermont. She just wasn't sure it was desirable.

"In this town, there are very few opportunities. If you are my age and you are not in college, and you don't have some sort of career, you're basically going to be stuck in a five-dollar-an-hour dead-end job. I didn't want that, so I went ahead and enrolled at the University of Vermont."

Susan adjusted to college-level academics more easily than she had expected, in part because she was not required to study the subjects that had plagued her in high school. "I have some learning disabilities, and they hit me hardest in math and languages, subjects that you just can't avoid in high school. I had to work very hard, and it was very stressful for me. I thought I would never make it in college—that I would fail out in my first year."

By the end of her sophomore year at UVM, financial realities caused Susan to think seriously about taking time off. "A lot of it came down to money. My brother had just finished school, which meant that I got less financial aid. Because my parents were no longer paying his tuition, the financial aid officer at UVM calculated that more of their income should now be available to pay UVM's tuition. My parents knew I was thinking about taking a year off, and they really believed it would be good for me."

Susan began to look around for things to do. "I was looking for an internship. I didn't have to make any money; I just couldn't spend any. I decided that what I truly wanted was to get involved with an environmental center that emphasized science more than just outdoor skills."

After compiling a long list of centers that interested her, Susan began making phone calls. "I didn't know about any of these places or what they were looking for. Some of them were really prestigious, and many of them wanted you to be a graduate student."

Susan found a job at Hobart Outdoor Center in Fairlee, Vermont. She began work there after spending the summer as a camp counselor.

"Hobart was such an amazing experience. It is set up for groups of schoolchildren that come for a few days at a time. Classes come, and the teachers break them up into groups of ten or twelve. Usually, the teachers put together kids who don't necessarily get along. So when they come to us, we set up challenges for them in an outdoor environment that they have to overcome as a group. Trust falls, a ropes course, teamwork exercises, things like that.

"Afterwards, we try to talk about it—what went right, how they felt in a particular role. If a kid is always the leader in the group, we try to get him to be a follower and get the follower to be the leader, just to get kids to experiment and think about how they treat each other.

"I think the best thing about the program was that all the staff that came in that year was new, and everyone was so excited to learn. I felt like I took in so much in so little time. It has given me the strength to deal interpersonally, which was a great experience to bring with me to what followed after that."

Susan's job at Hobart was only a two-month stint, and midway through her time there she had not found another job. At that point, she started looking back through her notes, and a place called the Breckenridge Outdoor Education Center caught her eye.

"When I first looked at the information, I had no idea that a large part of what they did there was teach disabled people to ski. I'd never worked with kids with disabilities before, and that really intimidated me. How would I react in a situation like that?

"One of the big reasons I decided to go was that they seemed so nice initially. They sent me information right away when I hadn't heard from all these other places at all, and when I called from Hobart to find out more, the woman I talked to was so nice.

"Then, after I knew I was going, I kept running into people who had done this internship. Everyone said, 'Definitely go, it will be the greatest experience of your life.' "

When Susan first interviewed for the Breckenridge internship over the phone, the staff there led her to expect the worst. "I was expecting six months of hell," she recalled. "My boss kept insisting what a tough job it was, telling me how cold it was, and that we lived in this cabin three miles from the nearest shower.

"I was actually a little disappointed when I got there and discovered that there was a town between my cabin and my shower and that the shower was at a health club. I was expecting to have to dig outhouses."

Susan lived in a cabin with all the other volunteers, who were mostly in their twenties and early thirties. The cabin was heated with wood, and the volunteers shared in the cooking duties.

When Susan arrived, she found that she was going to be living with Mandy, a woman about her age from the University of Michigan. "I was out skiing the day Mandy moved in. When I came back, all her stuff was there, her mountain bike, and her helmet. I just had this feeling that we were really similar people."

Susan quickly discovered that, for all they had in common, she and Mandy had important differences as well. "I was not expecting her to have only one leg. When she first walked in, I kind of gulped. Wow, was I surprised. At first, I wasn't sure how to treat her. I didn't know when or whether to ask her if she needed help, because I didn't want to offend her.

"But then I realized, 'Well, how am I going to know if I don't ask?' And so I would ask and take her word for it when she said, 'No, I don't want any help carrying this.' A lot of people in her life ask her if she needs help, and just asking doesn't make her angry. It's when they don't take her word for it when she says no that sets her off."

Breckenridge was like Hobart in that it also had an outdoor education/team-building course, but most Breckenridge interns spend at least eighty percent of their time on the slopes. Philosophically, the two places were very different.

"I'm the kind of person who is a nurturer, and my past work experiences really drew on those skills," Susan said. "The philosophy at Breckenridge is more to just let loose and have fun. There's definitely not any pity involved, no consoling.

They're really hard on their participants, in a good way. It's a real challenge."

At Breckenridge, Susan explained, the mountain was the great equalizer. "Everybody on skis is disabled, because everyone is a fool when they have these long fiberglass things on. Skiing for people who can't walk can be the most liberating, enlightening thing, because for a change they aren't fighting gravity. Gravity is finally helping them, and it's the one time they can really go fast," Susan said.

Susan was constantly learning more about what it was like to be physically disabled. "There was a blind woman who had done some teaching with us, and she had a disability dinner, where everyone was assigned a different disability. I was blind, some people didn't have limbs, and we had to work together to get the meal cooked.

"We ended up re-creating the disability dinner when a lot of our groups came up. It was great, because it opens up all this discussion about how you treat each other during the dinner, which leads directly into discussions of how people are treated, or want to be treated."

Groups of skiers came from all over the country, and each person presented unique challenges. "Every lesson was different, because every disability is different," Susan said.

"You just have to always be prepared to come up with a way to solve a problem. Whether it's a four-runner for a person in a wheelchair, or dealing with special equipment for limb losses, or acting as a guide for a blind skier, you have to be able to look at a situation and say, 'Okay, this is not working. How am I going to fix it?' "

In addition to room and board, Susan received a $50 monthly stipend, which she said was plenty. "There really wasn't a lot of stress. People took good care of us in town, invited us over for meals and things, because they thought we were doing such good work. And a lot of times the older students would want to take us out to bars, and to disco night."

Susan's time at Breckenridge was finite, since she knew she was going to work at a camp for the summer. "I used to dread going back to school," she said. "I would go to Boulder sometimes and look at the university there and get the willies. My job was so much more fun. I guess what I enjoyed most was coming home at night after teaching and just having that be **my** time and not having to stress about all this work."

When she returned to school, Susan found she had changed in unexpected ways. "I had always been a pretty quiet person, but in Colorado I went out more than I had ever done in my entire life," she said. "When I got back to school, I was definitely more social, meeting more people."

She also got herself out of the dorms. "I was living in an apartment with one of my friends from freshman year and two other women. I think that made all the difference in the world.

"The hardest part about coming back was the fact that the amount I learned during my time off—you can't even compare it to the type of things you learn in school," she said. "Now, in some ways, I feel like I'm just waiting out the rest of my time here."

Susan said that this problem was especially apparent in an English class she took her first semester back at UVM. "Whenever I went to work on my English, it was always to work on this one essay I was writing about Mandy," she said. "I really wanted to make that one right. I let all my other work in the class slack, and I ended up handing in an incomplete portfolio.

"I don't know how my grade will reflect that, and you know what? It doesn't really matter. I think I did what was important, and that's the most significant thing. That semester was where I processed my experience and my relationship with

Mandy—what it was, why it was important, and what I gained from being with her and being out there.

"My geography class that semester, and my geology class, sure, they were great. But will I ever use that information again? Probably not, no. I think that's part of what was so important about my year away. I will always use the things I learned."

LAURA CASTRO

San Diego, California
GROSSMONT JUNIOR COLLEGE '95

Indoor learning never held much appeal for Laura Castro. Though she was an honors student in junior high, a decided lack of effort and motivation marked her experience at San Diego High School. "I was in all advanced classes, but I was just too lazy to do the work," she recalled. "I would go home and I basically just wouldn't do anything."

Though Laura had a tough time putting her finger on the exact source of her malaise, her verdict on high school couldn't be clearer. "I just didn't like it at all," she said.

When it came time to decide what to do after high school, Laura wondered if going straight to college would be wise. "I realized that I was not going to do very well if I went to college with the same attitude I had in high school."

Laura also knew she would never want to be stuck working in an office from nine to five. "Ever since I can remember, I have wanted to be a wildlife biologist. I have loved animals and being outdoors all my life."

Her opportunities to pursue wildlife biology were limited by the cost of expensive summer enrichment programs that would have allowed her to explore the field. The summer before her senior year, however, she found paying work in a summer conservation corps near her home. Signing on for a full-time stint in the state's conservation corps seemed like a natural way for her to continue to explore a career in the outdoors.

The California Conservation Corps is proud of its unofficial motto: Hard work, low pay, and miserable conditions. "The recruiters don't tell you very much when you sign up," Laura recalled. "They don't want you to know how hard you're going to work."

Almost any California resident between the ages of eighteen and twenty-three is eligible. Most sign on for a year and rotate between several work centers all over the state. The centers serve as base camps for the small groups of young people that fan out to work in the state's parks and forests.

Corps members wear uniforms, get up with the sun, and often work late. For their efforts, they earn minimum wage and a small scholarship toward college. The corps is incredibly diverse from a demographic perspective, and most recruits enter with only a high school education or less.

Laura arrived for her two-week training session in October 1989 with high hopes but few expectations. The most immediate surprise, she said, was realizing how different she was from many of the other corps members. "Many of the people there were having problems at home and their parents forced them to join, or they were trying to get away from gangs, or their parole officer forced them to go. I was a little bit shocked."

The two weeks of training were intense. Laura learned to administer first aid, handle power tools, and fight fires—all things that she had never done before and had not expected to be doing. "They worked us hard. Up at dawn, running, then back for breakfast, then training all day long. The leaders were very mean, but we learned a lot."

For her first assignment, she spent seven months at the corps' Porterville Base Camp, near Sequoia National Park. From there, with her crew leader and a team of twelve, she maintained nature trails, cleared streams, and did other upkeep work in the state's national parks.

Though the crew came from a variety of backgrounds, group dynamics were no problem, according to Laura. "The only problem was the attrition rate, which is pretty high. People are coming and going a lot, so you just have to get used to new people coming in."

For Laura, however, being part of the group, especially after hours, was difficult for a variety of reasons. "It mostly had to do with my personality. I was very, very shy. I didn't really talk to anybody outside of work except my roommate for the first four months. I was very antisocial."

Eventually, however, as her crew members got to know her, they came to admire her. "I think the guys respected the fact that I worked really hard. When I finally started talking, I think it made a big difference in terms of their opinion of me."

After her seven-month stint at Porterville, Laura's group leader encouraged her to apply to a backcountry crew. Working backcountry for the CCC is like being a Green Beret in the Marines—it means you're the cream of the crop and you get sent out into the wild to tackle some of the toughest, most rewarding projects.

"At first I didn't really want to go to backcountry," she recalled. "People talk about it, how intense it is, and it seemed really scary to me. It was not so much living out in the woods as it was living with people I didn't know."

The backcountry lived up to its reputation. "Every day we'd wake up, get outside fast, hike into the woods fast, everything was fast, fast, fast. They were teaching us how to mark and fix trails, build stone steps, and make walls on the sides of trails."

The crew began moving around to different sites to work on various backcountry trails. Some locations were so remote that their food and supplies had to be brought in by mule. "It was fascinating," Laura recalled. "Each site, we got to do something different. The rock stairs were especially neat, because you were designing your own work. You had to find just the right rock, so it was like a puzzle. It was fun."

As her five-month backcountry stint wore on, Laura found that the experience was tougher mentally than it was physically. Once again, she said she found herself set apart from the group, though it was not her shyness this time.

"There was this guy there, a Forest Service supervisor actually, who wouldn't accept me because I was Catholic. He would make all these comments and try to get me to read books that painted a negative image of God. It was basically a prejudice.

"If it had just been him, it would have been fine, but he also got one of my crew members to bother me about it, and that was just too much for me to handle. I had never really had any problems with people before, and I didn't know how to defend myself very well."

As difficult as it was, however, the experience had its up side. "I had to learn to become more aggressive and assertive," Laura said. "I had never talked back to a superior before, but there I finally had to learn to just fight with him."

By the time backcountry ended, Laura's twelve months were up, but she petitioned for a longer stay in the corps and was allowed to continue for another year. She moved on to Elkhorn Slough, a much smaller CCC center near the Pacific Ocean, between Monterey and Santa Cruz.

There, she began an internship with a wildlife biologist. Her responsibilities included watering plants on nature trails, planting vegetation, clearing overgrown brush with a chain saw, constructing signs for the trails, and learning about the local wildlife.

Though the experience was interesting, Laura quickly realized that it was not the kind of wildlife biology she wanted to pursue as a career. "It confused me at first, because I didn't realize that not all wildlife biology is like that. I want to be out in the field, seeing animals in their natural environment. My boss spent a lot of time in his office."

After eight months at Elkhorn, Laura was selected to join a group of corps members and college students that would spend the next two months conducting a comparative ecological study of Lake Baikal in Siberia and Lake Tahoe.

For Laura, who had never left California before except to visit relatives who lived just over the border in Mexico, the experience was mindblowing. "Lake Baikal was absolutely beautiful," she said. "There are a lot of stereotypes about Siberia being all snowy and desolate, but the area around the lake is wonderful."

The students and CCC crew members studied with a group of Russian students in Siberia and then served as hosts when the group returned to study Lake Tahoe.

Laura finally left the corps a short time after she returned from Lake Tahoe. She started working as a teacher's aide in Santa Cruz in October 1991 and then returned to San Diego the next summer and found a similar job.

That fall, she also began taking classes at Grossmont Junior College near San Diego, with an eye toward getting her general education credits and a few basic science courses out of the way before transferring to an out-of-state school that had field-study programs for biology majors.

"I'm doing so well in school now it almost seems easy, or at least a lot easier than I thought it would be," she said. "It's so hard to explain, but I guess after all that time away just thinking about my academics and my future, I got motivated. I really enjoy school now."

Laura said that the extent to which her two years of hard labor changed her was shocking at first. But, she insists, she would hardly do anything differently if she had it to do over again.

The CCC is open only to California residents, but many states have developed similar programs under the National Service Bill. "Now," Laura said, "I try and convince everyone else to join the Corps, too."

KRISTIN ERICKSON

New York, New York

BROWN UNIVERSITY '96

As she approached her senior year at Brearley, a small private girls' school in New York City, Kristin didn't know where she wanted to go to college, or even if she wanted to go at all. Her parents, meanwhile, had aspirations of their own. "They made me look at schools like Harvard. I think that was because both of them grew up in small towns and had never had that kind of opportunity. This was their chance to go to Harvard."

When Kristin raised the idea of taking time off, "my parents freaked out a little bit," she said. "Ultimately, they said, 'Okay, but you have to have a complete plan.'"

Kristin sought assistance from Cornelius Bull, a highly regarded educational consultant whose Center for Interim Programs is based in Cambridge, Massachusetts. [See page 263 of Resources.]

Bull urged Kristin to look into being a courier for the Frontier Nursing Service in rural Appalachia. Founded in 1925, FNS is a health-care organization in Wendover, Kentucky, with a hospital and four outpost clinics. Originally, doctors visited the more remote areas on horseback. The mail took a long time to get there, and FNS volunteer couriers would bring mail to all the clinics. They still need people to deliver mail, and today's volunteers also help out with many other chores.

The application process was easy and straightforward, and FNS offered Kristin a spot. She left for Kentucky during the summer after high school, even though some New York friends were skeptical. "Oh, Appalachia," she remembers them saying. "Better bring your own toilet paper."

Kristin joined ten other couriers ages seventeen and up who were volunteering at FNS in exchange for room and board.

"I started going on home health rounds once a week. This woman Maybelline and I would spend the day driving around to people's homes. We bathed homebound patients who couldn't bathe themselves because they were old or disabled. Growing up in New York City, I saw a lot of intense, crazy things. But there was something very intimate about going into someone's home and bathing their body. There was a lot of trust involved in that.

"I gave a bath to this frail little guy married to a big-mama woman. He must have been ninety years old. They had something like sixteen kids together. One time we were walking and he points to his crotch and says, 'See that? Sixteen kids.' He was fantastic.

"You had to get to certain people every day, but there were days with fewer patients, so it never felt rushed. Sometimes you'd just end up sitting around drinking coffee and hanging out with a family.

"It could also be very depressing. In one home, the daughter went to work every day in nice clothes but the house was just crazy. When it was sprayed, they collected a five-pound bag of cockroaches."

Kristin spent a lot of her time just listening. "When I graduated from high school, I had all these fixed ideas about how I felt about this and what to do about that. And when I got to Kentucky, I just shut my mouth and listened. A lot of my organized high school ideas were tossed around and smashed. Which was great, but it was also confusing."

One of Kristin's favorite people was Sherman, an eighty-three-year-old craftsman who taught her how to build furniture out of walnut wood. "I used to go over to his house at six in the morning. We'd drink coffee and shoot the shit. I built a rocking chair with him. He'd always say, 'Women is the cause of all trouble.' And I'd say, 'Sherman, men is the cause of all trouble and you know it.' "

Kristin was at FNS through December, and she decided that she wanted to stay on. "I had been through enough compartmentalized experiences in my life. I didn't want to just up and go right when I was really getting into it."

Kristin continued to involve herself in a variety of projects. "I became friends with a woman named Lucile—everyone called her Thumper. She was a thirty-year FNS veteran and had started to lose her vision. She wanted to reread *Pilgrim's Progress*, but her eyes were all screwy. So I said, 'I'll read it to you,' which became a really fun thing to do."

Kristin's plan for the second half of her time off was to work on a farm in Pennsylvania. "I got room, board, and a small weekly stipend in return for working six days a week for ten or twelve hours a day at the farm. I was living in a barn, and my geography became pretty local while I was there. I worked with four other apprentices like myself."

The farm grew "all kinds of vegetables" and sold them to upscale markets and fancy restaurants in Philadelphia.

"One time, we all went into Philadelphia after a day of work and ate at one of the restaurants. Here we are, all of us with dirt under our fingernails and in the cracks of our skin no matter how hard we scrubbed. 'Yes, please, I'd like the special salad this evening.' And there were all these vegetables, beautifully arranged on the plate, which we had been cutting by the handful that afternoon, with a massive price on it. It was wild."

Kristin's schedule had a fair amount of regularity to it, since the farm had two delivery days a week. Of the four remaining workdays, two were for harvesting the crops for the next day's orders. "First thing in the morning, we'd go out and cut chives. Chives are all perky in the morning when they have dew on them, but later in the day they lose their moisture and get kind of limp."

"There was always way more work than we could possibly do. Sometimes there was something to be done and it would be Sunday, our day off. But plants don't observe Sundays. So, instead of baking my bread for the week, doing laundry, and lying by the creek, I would go out and do it.

"There is an incredible satisfaction that comes from working so hard physically on something and then **seeing** it. Once at the end of a long day, we were all tired and the sun was going down. And there were two thousand tomato plants left unplanted. 'But dammit,' we said, 'we were supposed to do it today, and those really should get into the ground—they're getting really big. Let's do it. Let's just load them up and go out to the field.'

"And we just did it. Plant and plant and plant and the sun goes down and you're still planting, planting, and then . . . stop, and they're there. Beautiful rows of tomato plants."

Kristin spent a lot of time alone in Pennsylvania. "It was solitude but not loneliness. After a long day, I didn't want to talk with anybody. I just wanted to make food, write a few sentences in my journal, and crash. It was a very focused time. My only goal was to write something every day in my journal. Sometimes the only entry would be 'Picked 100 quarts of strawberries today.' Then I'd pass out.

"I have a couple entries that just say 'Rain!' Sometimes people would come to the farm on a sunny day in the middle of a long dry spell and say, 'What a beautiful day.' We thought, 'Oh, yeah, beautiful day, everything's dying. It's great.' Rain was a godsend at times."

Kristin learned a lot from Mark, the farm's owner, who had taught agriculture in college for eighteen years. She felt she was "making up for a deficit of eighteen years spent living in a city. I was like a little kid running around asking questions. I feel lucky that Mark was so willing to answer my questions. Sometimes his answers just gave me more questions, though, and that is why I'm studying biology now."

Kristin left the farm at the end of the summer, in time to start Brown University. "It was hard to leave. I almost decided to stay through the harvest. When I was planning it, I thought, 'Oh, four months, what a nice long time to be on a farm.' But four months is nothing."

Leaving the farm reminded Kristin of a unicorn tapestry at the Cloisters, the medieval museum back in New York. "Of course, in the tapestry, all the plants are flowering at once. But the only way to see all the plants and flowers blossom in the garden is to spend four seasons there. My advice is, if you're going to be on a farm, be there for the whole year. No question. I didn't harvest what I planted and that made me feel something was very incomplete."

The college environment seemed "ludicrous" to Kristin when she first arrived. "I got the course catalogue, and looking through it, I saw courses in women's studies. I thought, 'Where's the men's studies department? What's going on here?'

"College feels to me like a very soft, cushy, and in some ways irresponsible environment. So much intellectualizing. An old teacher of mine was telling me to join all these various feminist organizations. I said, 'All I can control is myself. I'm in charge of myself, and I'm a woman.' I felt very strong and all the organizations seemed so far removed from the real world. I think my approach to things like that has become much more personal and less formulaic."

Kristin did find one course in the catalogue that she was excited about: " 'Plants, Food, and People.' It was plant biology and agriculture. My little academic harvesting."

Socially, Kristin made friends almost by accident. "When people first come to college, there is a whole mentality of 'Oh God, I have to have this intense camp experience. Let's all be best friends right now, this week.' Because we're all so unsure of ourselves.

"I didn't really throw myself into dorm life. I would just take off on my bike early in the morning and do my own thing. But in not looking for people, I collided with some remarkable folks."

Kristin has considered transferring or spending a year at another school. "Something I learned from being in Kentucky, though, is the value of staying in one place and really digging in. Sometimes, when people take time off, I think there's a certain urgency: 'Oh, I have to pack in all these tremendous wild experiences. I've always wanted to go to Nepal.' So people rush through a series of packaged three-month experiences. I think that's a shame.

"The things that interest me most are always underneath the surface. It takes a while to find that out, as in a relationship with someone. It could take a year to get past all that initial stuff.

"It's like digging down into the soil. There's so much going on, and you just keep seeing more."

Volunteering Abroad

RANDY LEWIS

Devon, Pennsylvania
COLLEGE OF WOOSTER '94

Randy Lewis first cut his teeth as an environmental activist on some troublemaking brownies.

"I was a bad, rotten kid. One time in middle school, my friend and I made brownies with a laxative in them and brought them to school to leave for all the teachers. We started bragging right away, and word spread. We got called into the principal's office and the brownies were sitting there on his desk.

"We told him that the whole thing had been a joke, and that they were just regular brownies. He said in that case we had a choice. We could eat the entire plate of brownies or he would call our parents and tell them about the joke. So we ate the entire plate, and spent the whole rest of the day in the bathroom."

After several similar stunts, Randy's parents decided he would be better off in boarding school. During his senior year, Randy's boarding school required each student to complete a month-long project before they graduated. "At the time, I had been reading a book about marine mammals. I decided to look further into it, and through my school I was able to go to the Woods Hole Oceanographic Institution in Massachusetts."

Working at Woods Hole opened Randy's eyes to a number of environmental issues that affected marine wildlife. "It was there that I first heard of the Sea Shepherd Conservation Society. A lot of people thought that they were terrorists, blowing up fishing boats and giving a bad name to the environmental movement. I was thinking, 'Wow, cool. These people are actually doing something.' I started reading a lot of environmental magazines and anything I could get my hands on about the Sea Shepherds."

Randy discovered that the Sea Shepherds refer to themselves as a marine mammal conservation society. They own a boat, which had gone on campaigns to fight the destruction of marine wildlife.

"I learned that they don't injure people, but they do sink ships after getting everyone off. To me, when someone is fishing using illegal or harmful methods, sinking their boat is just like taking a gun away from a person who is about to shoot someone. Violence is hurting another sentient being, not destroying property."

When it came time to apply to college, Randy borrowed a page from the Metamucil fallout. "I stuck a roll of toilet paper into the typewriter and wrote my college application essay on it. I wrote about a guy who got stuck in the bathroom and had to eat tubes of toothpaste to stay alive. Some of my friends were applying to the College of Wooster in Ohio, so I applied there, and I guess it worked."

Randy arrived at Wooster and found that it was a lot like boarding school, minus the rules. "I did a lot of partying. It was a fun year. I didn't have any real clear goals in mind academically."

After a brief flirtation with being a music major, Randy settled on English. "I saw it as being the most flexible. I thought that maybe I could become a writer about environmental issues, but I was still basically floating around and going through the motions.

"By my sophomore year, I began to think more about what I was going to do when I graduated. I realized that I wasn't getting anything out of school, and I thought it would be a good idea for me to get out into the real world for a while."

Randy's parents were not averse to him spending some time away from the classroom, but they didn't want him sitting in their living room all year either. "They gave me a deadline to figure something out. The deadline was the good healthy push I needed.

"I decided to call up Sea Shepherds just to check. They sent me this whole crazy application. They wanted to know if I had any police or detective experience, or if I had ever been in the FBI. They've been infiltrated before, so they were worried, I think. They also asked me if I had my own gas mask. I found out later that no one needs to bring his own gas mask. They just ask that to weed people out.

"I answered, 'No, no, no,' to every question, thinking I had no chance. I didn't hear anything back, so I called up and I actually ended up talking to the captain, Paul Watson. He told me that the ship was down in Norfolk, Virginia, and that I should feel free to go down and take a look.

"I kind of misinterpreted him to mean that I was on the boat. He probably thought I would take one look, get scared, and leave. But I threw all my stuff into the car, drove on down, and got on board. I told the four people working on the ship that the captain had sent me down, and I went to work cleaning the boat and painting.

"The captain came down right before the ship was scheduled to leave. It takes a lot to faze him. He talked to the crew about me, and then just said, 'Okay, you're on.' I found out later that they had a stack of applications three feet high. The whole application process is unnecessary. What you need to do is go to it and show them you're a hard worker. Luckily, that's what I did."

The Sea Shepherds are supported by 20,000 members, some of whom are wealthy industrialists who donate large sums of money anonymously. The donations go toward feeding the crew and maintaining the ship—a large task, considering it eats $20,000 in diesel fuel alone on each campaign.

The ship's first destination was the Bahamas. "The captain always keeps the location of the campaign a secret, to prevent media leaks. I thought we were going up to Iceland to sink whaling boats, so I was excited to find out that we were going south instead," Randy said.

"We are a very intimidating ship. The boat is all black, and on the side is a huge steel I-beam sharpened to a point that sticks out from the side. We call that the can opener, and we use it to ram ships. We had a water cannon on board that used to be connected to huge barrels of government-issued custard. We also had butyric acid to throw onto other ships—super-stinky stuff.

"We have Kevlar helmets and vests, in case people start shooting at us, and we have guns on board. Before I was on, they had knives thrown at them by Japanese drift-netters. It's for real. When you head out, you know you might not be coming back, and they outline that to you very clearly before you leave."

The ship sailed to Key West to refuel before setting out on Randy's first wildlife-protection campaign. "We were planning to hunt some purse-seiners off of Mexico. They are tuna fishermen, and tuna tend to hang out under pods of dolphins. These guys find the dolphins and then wrap a huge net around the entire pod. Dolphins are pretty much blind, so they set off underwater explosives to deafen them so they don't move, and the tuna stay put. Then they pull the net in like the drawstrings of a purse.

"They end up pulling in lots of dolphin as well as tuna. The monofilament nets catch the fins of some of the dolphins and tear them off. Dolphins tend to live and hunt in social groups, so even those that get away by themselves starve."

After traveling through the Panama Canal, Randy's ship encountered an even worse sight while sailing north off the coast of Costa Rica. "Boats in protected waters were catching dolphins and cutting them up to throw back in the water as bait for shark. They would catch the shark, cut its fin off, throw the shark back in the water, and send the fin to Japan for shark fin's soup, which is supposed to be an aphrodisiac.

"They were in wooden ships, so if we rammed them, they would have splintered apart. So we threw grappling hooks at them, took their nets away, and threw rum bottles full of butyric acid at them. One drop in an office building can cause the whole place to be evacuated, so they weren't going anywhere for a while. We alerted the Costa Rican government, and they were really thankful. They actually asked us to stay and keep patrolling, but we told them no, we had things to do."

The ship sailed north once more and eventually encountered, not Mexican, but American purse-seiners. "This was supposedly a dolphin-safe tuna company, and they were so blatant. We went in to try to ram them, but they were faster than we were. We had a smaller, faster ship with us that was able to go in and get really good pictures, though.

"For every one boat you ram, there are hundreds more. We were one tiny ship up against an armada of destruction. But when you get footage like we did, that's something that will get on TV. You'll be sitting in a bar and you'll see it, and say, 'What the hell? Who is that?' That's how widespread change can happen.

"That was one thing that the captain taught me. He is really media-savvy. Never before has one individual or small group been able to command the attention of the entire world."

The ship docked in Southern California for a few weeks and then set out on its longest campaign since Randy had come on board. "We were going up to the North Pacific to confront some Japanese drift-netters. They lay out thirty-five to forty miles of net. It's monofilament net, so the birds and the fish can't see it, and anything that touches it gets caught. It's not fishing—they're raping the ocean, and it's a sick, sick thing.

"We were up near the Aleutian Islands, and we were going to search until the fuel ran out. The Pacific is much bigger than the Caribbean, so we were in an even worse situation trying to find these boats, but after several false calls, we found them.

"We were a few miles away from them, and we started pulling in their net as they were laying it out. Their nets cost about a million dollars apiece, so one of our goals was always to try to get their net, in addition to ramming their ship. But we hadn't foreseen the fact that their net would get completely stuck on our propeller.

"It was one in the morning, and the swells were hitting our ship. We couldn't go anywhere, and we were in serious trouble, because if the swells got any worse and we couldn't

turn the propeller on, the boat would turn and we could cap-
size and drown.

"One of my duties on the boat was chief diver, and I had
to go down and clear the propeller. We didn't even have a
diving knife. I just grabbed a steak knife from the kitchen.
Someone came down with me to hold a light, and I got in the
cage that held the propeller, which was about as big as I am.
The boat was bucking so bad that the propeller was coming
out of the water, and I kept slamming my head against the hull.
The light was bobbing up and down, and I basically had to do
the whole thing by feel.

"I finally got it clear, and then I got caught in the monofilament. It's like quicksand. The more you struggle, the more
you get snagged, and then the other guy got caught, too. I
didn't even panic, I just figured I was going to die. Thank God
we both did the right thing. We were able to relax and float
up to the surface, and they came in with the small boat and
cut us free. It was the closest brush with death I've ever had."

They managed to pull in a few miles of net that night, and
the next morning they moved in to ram the ship. "We had
made radio contact and told them that what they were doing
was illegal. We had deliberately timed the campaign to coincide
with an international moratorium on drift-netting, but the
United Nations doesn't do anything. We were the only ones
out there enforcing it.

"We circled them a few times, made a few rushes at them,
and turned away at the last moment, just toying with them. Then
we moved in and called them on the radio and said, 'Prepare to
be rammed!' It was going to be a direct hit, really hard, but as we
were about to hit them, some guy comes out on their deck walking toward where we were going to hit them. We turned away
at the last moment, and it ended up being a sort of glancing blow,
but the crunch was still pretty incredible."

Once again, the Sea Shepherds were outrun, as the Japanese ship retreated. Randy and the crew turned around to head for Canada, but they were stopped almost immediately. "The Japanese had told the American government that we were throwing Molotov cocktails at their ship, so we were intercepted by the Coast Guard. Some people came on board and interrogated every one of us. I think they were from the FBI, but they never identified themselves. They started asking me all these questions, like whether I was an anarchist, whether I believed in God, and whether I thought there should be a revolution. I said, 'Look, I'm just out here trying to protect marine wildlife.'"

Randy managed to make it back to North America without getting arrested, and he toyed with the idea of not returning to school. "We were going to go up and sink whalers in Iceland, but that campaign was delayed. It was close to September at that point, and I had already finished two years of school. I knew if I didn't go back then, I probably never would.

"Coming back was really hard. I'd been out at sea for a year, living such an adventure, and each day at school seemed so boring. Every person seemed so boring—just the sameness of them all. I thought I had made the wrong choice.

"Then all of a sudden it happened, real quick. I realized that what I really wanted to do was change my major to something more environmentally focused, maybe environmental science. I looked into it and found that nothing like it existed at the college.

"So I started talking to a biology professor, and she was a big help. She told me that if I wanted to do it on my own, I would have to take certain classes. I got the degree requirements from other schools that had an environmental science major, and I developed a program of my own.

"I was going to have to take biology, chemistry, geology,

and then take political science classes to balance it out. It was an incredibly burdensome schedule, but I realized, if I was going to be there, why not make the best of it? I knew by then that I wanted to go into environmental work, so I just focused on that, and I worked harder than I had ever worked in school before.

"I came across a lot of opposition. The school was going through some cutbacks, and I think the last thing they needed was someone designing a major that other people would want to do—so they would have to create another department. Some professors didn't think it was a serious enough pursuit, and some others didn't think I would get enough depth. But I went on and graduated, and I was the first person ever to graduate from my school with an environmental science major. Near the end, people came up to me to find out how they could do the same thing. I left a legacy."

While Randy believes that more people should consider taking time off, he said that any activist should think hard about what he or she is prepared to endure for a cause. "There are so many people I would not recommend Sea Shepherds to. There were people who came on the boat at one stop and got right off at the next. Some people should be working in Washington talking to politicians. You've got to do whatever your calling is.

"It was a hard life out there, but there is nothing like sitting out on the front deck when a pod of dolphins starts riding the bow wave of your ship. I looked down at them once, and one turned on its side, waved with his flipper, and jumped up to the point where I could nearly touch him. Almost as if to say, 'Hey, thanks for what you're doing.' Experiences like that, I wouldn't trade for the world."

ERIN HURME

Pullman, Washington

UNIVERSITY OF WASHINGTON '96

Erin Hurme knew she wanted to explore her Christian faith more thoroughly than she had been able to in high school. All she needed was a means to do so.

"I didn't fit in very well at the small, private, and excessively spiritual Christian high school I graduated from in 1992," she said. "My world and its God were small and legalistic. I knew there had to be more to life than school and pain. And I knew that I had to get away."

When she was sixteen, Erin won a scholarship to train with the Seattle Children's Theater. Shortly thereafter, they asked her to join the company. "I started to dress differently from people at my school and was hanging out with friends who were gay. A big no-no," she said.

A family friend encouraged Erin to apply to an international nondenominational missionary organization known as Youth with a Mission. YWAM requires would-be missionaries to attend Discipleship Training School to prepare for their work in the field.

Erin asked to attend a DTS base in Canada where she would be able to combine her interest in theater with Christianity. The program she applied to prepared graduates to perform a religiously inspired drama as part of their missionary work. The group was scheduled to train from September through January before going on a two-month mission to Honduras. After being accepted, Erin immediately started to fundraise to pay for the experience. "YWAM is well known within Christian circles, which made my job easier," she said.

Erin gave a speech at her church explaining her desire to do missionary work and asked for support. She needed to pay DTS and YWAM $4,000 to cover tuition, room, and board, and she required an additional $2,000 for personal expenses during her seven-month experience.

"I searched all over to find people who would sponsor me," she said. "Let's say you need $1,000 a month for six months. You need to go out and find twenty people willing to pay you $50 a month. Or forty people willing to pay you $25 a month."

To thank the members of her church and the other people who supported her, Erin promised to write her sponsors a newsletter detailing her experiences during missionary training and while working in Honduras.

In September, Erin flew to the DTS base in Cambridge, Ontario, a town forty-five miles outside of Toronto, for four months of hard training. "I awoke the first morning and found myself thrown into a cultural patchwork quilt," she recalled.

Erin's group included fifty-five people from ten different countries and thirty-five different religious backgrounds, between seventeen and thirty-five years of age. "We're talking serious diversity," she said. "That multiracial, multiethnic, cross-cultural diversity appealed to me because I am of Caribbean ethnicity and felt limited by my largely white, upper-middle-class, strictly Pentecostal high school."

Erin's daily schedule was grueling. "We were up every day at 6:30 and kept going full speed ahead until eight at night," she said. "You're living on top of everybody from the moment you wake up to the moment you go to bed."

Each day began with lectures in the morning. After lunch, everyone was assigned to work detail. "I got kitchen duty," she said, "and every day after lunch I had to scrub all the pots and pans for two hours."

Keeping a journal provided Erin with a chance to reflect privately on her experiences. "I've gone back and read my journal entries," she said, "and the number-one theme in the beginning was 'This sucks.'

"Every week we had a new speaker come in and talk for the entire week on a particular aspect of our faith. 'Why does evil exist?' for example. YWAM was very good about not shoving a particular brand of faith down our throats—sometimes the speakers would contradict each other. There were also daily group worship sessions, sometimes with music and singing."

After a brief recess for Christmas, the group reconvened for their trip to Central America. "We drove from Cambridge, Ontario, to New Orleans, Louisiana, and then flew on Honduras's national airline. We nicknamed it 'Stay at Home, Stay Alive.' "

Erin's missionary team stayed in a mountain village about three hours outside the capital city. Erin and some members of her group spoke Spanish, but others relied on a translator who traveled with them.

"Our village was in the middle of a verdant, lush valley that reminded me of a coffee commercial. All fifty-five of us slept

on a stone floor in the village meeting house. We had no running water, electricity, or indoor plumbing. We had to scrub
our clothes by hand in a big washtub."

Erin said it took her some time to get used to her new
living quarters. "When we went to the bathroom at night, we
had to go in buddies; one of us would be flicking the flashlight
to look for tarantulas and scorpions. In the mornings, I got up
at dawn and took a bucket bath with cold water."

The missionary group was divided into two teams, the
mime team and the work team. The work team helped the
townspeople build a new goat farm, as goat's milk was the area's
economic mainstay. "We were not just telling people 'God
loves you.' We were also trying to meet their needs on a practical level," she said.

Erin's experience in theater earned her a spot on the mime
team. The mime team traveled through all the neighboring
towns and villages and performed a one-hour interpretation of
the Christian Gospel. "We carted around speakers, a generator,
makeup, costumes, everything. The soundtrack was prere-
corded in Spanish, so all the villagers could understand it. The
performance was designed to spread the good news about Jesus
and the Christian faith," she said.

Erin found that her team's impact did not meet her expectations. "We assumed that the Hondurans would flock to us
and we would be like Billy Graham. It was a shock to find that
people didn't want to know anything about us or our Christianity. It was hard when we came home and people said, 'How
many people became Christians? Tons?' And we had to say,
'No, more like four or five, maybe.' "

Erin vividly remembers one encounter with an old peasant
woman who came up to her in tears after one of their per-
formances. "She was poor and came to me with no shoes on
and asked me to pray with her. She wanted to become '*una*

amiga de Jesus,' a friend of Jesus. I read a prayer and she kept on crying as she repeated the words out loud with absolute sincerity.

"I thought, 'If I came down here for just this one person, the trip was totally worth it.' Even though my rudimentary Spanish limited our conversation, I decided it's better to have a heart with no words than words without a heart."

At the same time, Erin forced herself to examine her own motivations. "Was I in Central America working to improve these people's lives because I genuinely cared for their welfare? I wasn't sure how much of my motivation came from being American, Christian, or simply myself, Erin."

After returning home and working for the summer, Erin enrolled at the University of Washington, where she is currently majoring in drama.

Although she missed the intensity and camaraderie of her group when she came home, she also knew she was not ready to commit herself to life as a missionary. "YWAM can become a life-style. I didn't want that, because then I would just be substituting one form of narrowness for another," she said.

Erin said she was originally looking for a divine, mystical experience with God, something akin to a vision of a burning bush or a parting sea. "What I set out to find was not really what I found. It was not my Christianity that I found—it was people."

BLAKE KUTNER

Palo Alto, California
DARTMOUTH COLLEGE '94

Though Blake Kutner and his family sometimes struggled to pay for Dartmouth, funding his time off was no problem at all.

As sophomore summer approached, Blake was studying Hebrew. His teacher told him about the Barnett Grant, a $2,000 award Dartmouth made available once per quarter. Apparently, no one had applied for it in four years.

"The award was given to students who wanted to work on programs promoting Arab–Jewish conflict resolution. Working with people directly was crucial. I found a program called Interns for Peace, which brings Arab and Jewish schoolchildren together for cultural exchanges. It fit the grant perfectly, and I applied for and got it."

Going to Israel began to look more and more like the right thing to do. "Everything gets all broken up after sophomore year, because people are constantly leaving to study abroad and coming back. I had heard that junior year was kind of a nothing year. People are getting kind of serious, but they're not on their way anywhere yet. It seemed like a good time to roll. I had no fear of falling behind. Taking time off from school is the difference between forty-two and forty-three years in the work force."

Interns for Peace normally requires a two-year commitment, but Blake wrote them anyway and asked to spend just four months with them. The coordinators were hesitant to sign him on. They told him it takes a while to get programs started in Israeli schools, and that continuity in leadership is essential. Requirements aside, Interns for Peace decided not to turn away a willing volunteer.

"I wrote back and said, 'Look, I have this grant, and it won't cost you a thing. My Hebrew is decent, I'll pay my rent, and I'll do whatever you need me to do to help out.' They finally said, 'Why not?' "

Blake told the people who ran the program that he would see them in February and then set his sights on New Orleans, where he planned to live with his uncle for a few months.

New Orleans did not disappoint. "My uncle knew everything and every person in New Orleans. He knew where the best holes in the wall were to eat, which musicians were hip and who was cool to see live. I did all of it. There was nothing to stop me."

Blake's uncle lived with another man, which itself was an education. "There was a lot of compromise involved, on both parts. The transformation from a household of two forty-five-year-old gay men to two forty-five-year-old men and one twenty-year-old slob . . . Well, it definitely had its ups and downs.

"When I moved in, I didn't have a very good idea of what a gay relationship was like. I had also never experienced real prejudice before until we went to look at houses one day and

I saw the way we were treated. Now I'm so much more aware of it at Dartmouth, where prejudice against homosexuals has always been abundant."

Blake's uncle, who is a doctor, helped Blake find a job as a lab assistant at the Louisiana State University Medical Center. The job involved growing bacteria as part of a study of German pollutants. "The job was fairly menial, but I ended up being excited to come to work every day anyway. I worked with this real hick guy and a woman from some random suburb. We listened to Rush Limbaugh every day. It was like I was in a totally different world."

At night, Blake handed out daiquiri samples and became intimately acquainted with the seamy side of New Orleans's French Quarter. "Many of our customers were strippers, and it was clear how slimy and racist the real New Orleans could be. At my bar, the white people out in front served drinks, and all the blacks were in the back, mixing the big frozen vats."

Shortly before Mardi Gras, Blake quit his job. After spending a few days enjoying and then recovering from the festivities, he packed up and left for Israel.

When he arrived, Interns for Peace had a room waiting for him in an apartment in a run-down neighborhood of Tel Aviv. The program paid for his apartment in what he described as "the Harlem of Israel," though he said the rent would not have amounted to more than $100 a month.

"Living there was incredible. My apartment was in a very poor neighborhood. The area was bombed during the Gulf War, and a lot of what used to be there isn't there anymore. I learned that many first- and second-generation Israelis in the neighborhood had come to Israel from Arab countries where they were harassed because of their Judaism."

Blake also enrolled in an ulpan, an intensive Hebrew course

that he remained in throughout his stay. At the same time, Interns for Peace essentially told him to create his own program for the next three months.

"When I called and told them I would do anything they wanted, they initially suggested teaching sports, setting up games between Jewish and Arab schools, and teaching English, all of which sounded like great things to do."

Blake realized that by the time he established a sports program it would be time to leave and that there might not be anyone after him to continue running it. So, instead, he concentrated on facilitating visits between schools and teaching English.

"I started by contacting several schools and offering my teaching services. That was great for the Arab schools, since they were short on teachers. Compared to the Jewish teenagers I met, who were basically fluent in English, the Arab kids knew very little English. They knew the most random assortment of stuff, like the names of all the World Wrestling Federation people."

Early on in his stay, Blake also went to a nearby Jewish community council and offered to teach English to new immigrants. In return, they arranged for him to have Sabbath dinner with a family every week. "They were Yemenite Jews, and they were unlike any families I had ever come into contact with. The kids were trying as hard as they could to modernize. All they wanted to talk about was *Melrose Place* and Burt Reynolds. The parents were about two thousand years behind them."

Blake said he gained the keenest appreciation of the problems facing Israeli society from observing the interaction between Jewish and Arab schoolchildren. Convincing the students to participate in the programs he organized was often difficult. "Some of the Jewish kids think they will be struck down by lightning if they enter a mosque, and vice versa. It's incredible," Blake said.

"You can tell that the Jewish kids come from the dominant segment of society by the way they behave. They are always louder and rowdier, and sometimes they are rude. We brought one group to an Arab school, and they refused to play with the Arab kids. We had some very unsuccessful exchanges.

"But there were other times when it was truly amazing. Some of the schools met four or five times, and the kids actually got to know one another and were hugging one another when they greeted. I have pictures of one girl in a full Arab headdress squatting next to a Jewish girl, and they're planting a tree together.

"When you see these kids, you realize how much the adults could learn from them. At some point, about age twelve or thirteen, the Jewish kids begin to understand, without really knowing why, that they are not supposed to like these people—that Arabs are bad.

"At the heart of the conflict, I think, is not the conflict over land or that Islam is fundamentally anti-Semitic. It's that people are brought up and reared to believe that there is a problem in Israel and that the other group of people is causing it. Seeing the kids together brings hope for the Israel to come."

While still in New Orleans, Blake had arranged the last leg of his overseas adventure. "I had read about this guy in *Runners' World* and *Sports Illustrated*. He's probably the world's foremost exercise physiologist. When I first wrote to him, he was conducting a study of why black and white athletes excelled in different sports. It's basically a taboo subject in the U.S., and I thought it was very interesting.

"I was thinking I might finish the pre-med requirements at some point, and I had taken some biology and chemistry and done fine. So I wrote him and did the same thing I did with

Interns for Peace, which was to convince him that it wouldn't cost him anything.

"I told him I would be willing to take the trash out—do anything, whatever lab work he needed, which is basically what he ended up using me for."

Blake arrived in Sweden at the end of June, after doing some traveling. "It turns out that people in some European countries take all of July off every year. I had no idea when I showed up. Everyone had just assumed that I knew. The third day that I was there, they literally said, 'Well, unless you have any better ideas, we'll see you in a month, because there's nothing here for you to do that you'll understand.' So I went to Turkey and Greece for the month of July.

"When I got back, I dove head-first into the lab work. It was pretty menial—I was basically pulling apart rat hearts and separating them under this little microscope and doing similar work with human thigh muscles.

"The things going on around me were incredible. They didn't have any particular goals for me to meet—there were thousands of these little rat hearts—so I could do as much or as little work as I wanted and as much or as little peering over people's shoulders as I wanted. Literally everything that went on in this lab ended up in some book or journal, so I just kept my eyes open.

"I didn't know what everything meant, and I only got to meet the researcher three times. But everyone I have talked to in scientific and academic communities has told me that the chance to work in his lab was the opportunity of a lifetime," Blake said.

Blake lived in a dorm room at the University of Stockholm, which was about the only living arrangement he could afford. When he moved back into Dartmouth's dormitories right after Labor Day, school did not live up to his expectations. "All there was to do on Friday night was go to the fraternity parties. The school wasn't evolving in the same way that I was. It was deevolution.

"The hardest part about returning was the feeling that I should do something with all these incredible things I had learned. I was a whole new man—I had eaten sheep's testicles—and then I came back to school, and it seemed like it was all for naught."

KARA NELSON

Corvallis, Oregon

UNIVERSITY OF CALIFORNIA AT BERKELEY '94

Kara Nelson's first chance to explore her interest in developing countries came when she realized that Mexico was right in her own back yard. "One day in high school, I realized, 'Wow, there is this incredibly poor country right next to mine and I've never been there.'"

To celebrate her graduation from high school in Corvallis, Oregon, Kara and her mother took a three-week trip to Mexico. They traveled Lonely Planet style, in the spirit of the popular low-budget travel guides published by Lonely Planet Publications. "We stayed in hotels where the Mexicans stayed and took regular Mexican buses. At the time, I thought what we were doing was crazy, that we were crossing the boundaries of traditional tourism. Of course, when I look back on it now, it's pretty tame compared to my subsequent traveling experiences."

Before she had another chance to travel in a developing country, Kara enrolled at the University of California at Berkeley. She was excited to begin school and had no fear of getting lost in the crowd. A strong science background in high school made a physics major at Berkeley a likely choice for her.

Classes were not as difficult as she thought they would be, which turned out to be a mixed blessing. "I just crammed before each test and got A's or B's. It took me a long time to recover from the bad study habits I developed."

A growing interest in radical politics and an active social life also affected Kara's attitude toward her studies. "There was just so much going on all the time. Every single day, there were protests on campus. There was an organization for every cause that you can imagine, and for causes that you've never heard of, even if you think you've heard of everything.

"I felt like America was damaging the entire rest of the world, and that most people didn't even know it. I grew up with this great life of incredible material affluence, in comparison with how most people around the world live. Unfortunately, I had no knowledge of the impact my life was having on the rest of the planet.

"At the same time, my physics classes just started getting less and less relevant to any of my life interests. The people in my classes were really lame. I just couldn't relate to most of them."

Feeling frustrated with both her academics and her extracurricular activities, Kara began to explore other options. Her first idea, a formal study-abroad program, did not meet her needs. "I was really sick of school and didn't know what I wanted from it. So, if I was going to take time off, I certainly didn't want to be in school."

Kara had always wanted to learn French, which inspired her to look into studying abroad, in West Africa. Her interest in Africa combined with a desire to volunteer in a development organization led her to the former British colony of Zimbabwe.

When exploring her options, Kara found some of the most

valuable information and resources right on Berkeley's campus. "All colleges have international connections. There are so many people around who have been to other countries, whether for academic reasons, personal interest, or because that's where they're from. You have to reach out and talk to those people."

Kara still needed to earn enough money to finance her trip, so she went back to Corvallis, home of Oregon State University. "I ended up putting up flyers all over the OSU campus in all the science departments. The flyers said I had lab experience and that I just needed to work for a little while. I found two jobs in two different labs. I worked at one in the morning and at the other in the afternoon. I really wanted to go to Africa."

Kara's hard work paid off and she was soon on her way to Harare, Zimbabwe. When she stepped off the plane, it took her a moment to get her bearings.

"There I was, trying to figure out how to get to a city that I couldn't even see, and two women walked up to me and said, 'Wow, we really like your shoes.' "

Kara told them that she had come to Zimbabwe for four months and hoped to volunteer for an aid organization. Because it had been difficult to make arrangements with aid organizations from home, Kara hoped she would be able to find a volunteer opportunity once she arrived. She also explained that she planned to stay at the youth hostel in Harare. " 'You can't stay at the youth hostel for four months,' they said. 'What are you thinking?' "

Kara shared a cab ride into the city with the two women and dropped her belongings off at their apartment. The Zimbabweans then took Kara to meet two British men who were working with a social service organization named Toc-H.

"Toc-H ran a number of racially mixed hostels in Harare, mostly for old white army veterans and young black men from rural areas who were studying in the city. In return for living there, the hostel's residents were required to do social work," Kara explained.

On her first day in Zimbabwe, the two British men took Kara to an orphanage for children who were missing one or more limbs. "The orphanage was out in a high-density suburb, a euphemism for slum, and there were kids without legs dragging themselves around on the ground and kids without arms who couldn't feed themselves. We threw them a party, with soda and cake, guitars, singing, dancing, and hanging out. It was me, the two British guys, the two Zimbabwean women I'd met at the airport, and a bunch of Zimbabweans who lived at the hostel."

When Kara checked back in with her friends from the airport, they already had a place for her to live. "I arrived at their apartment and they said, 'Oh, we arranged for you to live with our friend Anne.' Anne was an incredibly empowered woman in her own way. She went to vocational training school to become a lithographer and was the first woman in Zimbabwe ever to go through that training program."

When she looked into finding a teaching job, Kara ran into a ferocious bureaucracy. "Even though they desperately needed science teachers, at any level, in any school, I found so many things getting in the way."

She also looked into volunteering with one of the many nongovernmental organizations operating in Zimbabwe. "None of the NGOs wanted me. They need an incredible amount of time to initiate a volunteer into their organizations, and to actually get you to the point where you can be useful doing something. I realized that you can't just go over there and then all of a sudden make great things happen. You need to make a serious commitment and it takes a long time."

Kara's persistence paid off, however, and she finally discovered a unique volunteer opportunity. After the country's independence from British rule, Zimbabwe's mostly rural, extended-family-based society was under strain from increasing urbanization and industrialization. "Because of the independence war, a lot of people were left homeless and landless and familyless, and they all started migrating to the city. A mass-education policy in rural areas increased the number of people who migrated from the countryside to look for better jobs in the city."

The British people Kara met upon arriving in Harare put her in contact with a community of homeless people who had taken over some sprawling fields on the edge of town. "The squatters went around to different service organizations, especially churches, and got them to donate things, like blankets, clothing, and black plastic to use for tents. They would also get restaurants to give them food once a week. The area was basically a shantytown. The squatters elected a group of people to represent them in their lobbying effort to get the government to give them agricultural land on which to resettle. The Lancaster Agreement—which said there would be no land distribution in the first ten years following independence—had expired.

"They also decided to start their own school. The kids couldn't go to a regular school, since they didn't have a permanent address. So I offered to help start the school. It was super-informal. We would sit under a big tree. We had a broken blackboard that they had gotten somewhere, with a big crack through the middle of it. Sometimes we had chalk or pencils and paper.

"When I arrived in the morning, all the kids would see me and come running out to hug me. 'Kara's here, Kara's here.' Everyone would get all excited and the adults would say,

'Schooltime, it's schooltime.' Adults who didn't know English would come and sit in on my classes."

Kara's students ranged in age from near-infants to girls fifteen or sixteen. "The oldest boys were nine or ten, because by the time they were teenagers, most boys would go into town all day, either to beg for spare change or to wash windows and parked cars."

Kara was also learning to play the mbira, a Zimbabwean thumb-piano, and studying the Shona language at the local adult college. As for whether it was hard to make friends, "I was more plagued by having too many people that wanted to be my friend."

Kara ended her time in Zimbabwe with some solo travel to nearby Malawi, passing through war-ravaged Mozambique on the way. "Oh my God, it's so sketchy. I can't believe I did that."

She traveled what is known as the "gun run," where each day the armies from Zimbabwe and Malawi escort a convoy of trucks through the Tete corridor. The corridor runs through Mozambique and connects Zimbabwe with Malawi. "The convoy goes through once a day in each direction. Anyone can go through, but no one does it besides truck drivers and a few crazy people in private cars.

"On the way there, I ended up getting a ride with this totally racist white South African family. They were scared South Africa was being taken over by the blacks, so they were going to go and live in the bush in Malawi and make their own world. Super-weird.

"The whole road was completely blown up because land mines had been planted everywhere. The saddest part was the town of Tete, which was completely cut off from the rest of the world because of the war. There's absolutely nothing there, just thousands of starving people.

"There were hundreds and hundreds of people lining the streets when the convoy arrived, coming up to you. They were trying to sell you things that they had gotten from some aid organization, like men's button-down shirts, that were of no use to them. They needed food or fuel, they didn't need a button-down shirt."

On the way back, Kara rode with a truck driver. "The convoy was scheduled to leave at dawn but was postponed by policemen and soldiers gesticulating madly. I found out later that, the day before, the convoy had been attacked. No one on the convoy had been killed, but the army went after the rebel soldiers and killed four of them. The truck driver told me, 'No big deal, I do this all the time.' I thought, 'Oh my God, I'm going to die.' "

One of Kara's biggest shocks upon returning to the United States was rediscovering America's aversion to talking about race. "In Zimbabwe, it's a given that they live in a racist society. The white people discriminated against the black people. It's true, it happened, it still exists, and it's okay to talk about it. In the United States, we have this false image that everything is hunky-dory and that we don't live in a racist society anymore."

When she came back to Berkeley, Kara tried to pick up where she had left off, enrolling in the second semester of quantum mechanics and working to complete her physics major. "We spent five weeks trying to get an approximate solution to one equation for the motion of one atom. I started thinking that what I really wanted to do was work in developing countries and work with the environment."

Kara decided to become an environmental engineer and changed her major to biophysics. She has since graduated and is currently pursuing a Ph.D. in environmental engineering at the University of Washington.

"It's crazy how in this country people can go to school starting when they're five and have a Ph.D. by the time they're twenty-five or twenty-six without having any idea what the real world is like. And they get out and they don't know how to do anything besides go to school."

PART FOUR

Traveling in the United States

TED CONOVER

Denver, Colorado

AMHERST COLLEGE '81

$\mathbf{A}$s a college kid riding the freight trains with railroad hoboes twice his age, Ted Conover often stuck out.

When he tried to explain, half truthfully usually, what he was doing, the tramps generally took him at his word. "Well, I used to be a student at a college out East, but I grew tired of that life. I heard there were still guys riding the rails, and that had always seemed pretty interesting to me, so I thought I'd come check it out for myself," he told them.

Early on in his adventure, however, one reflective tramp caught the irony. "Young man," he said, laughing, "*this* will be your education!"

Ted was twenty-two when he left Amherst College in 1980 to ride the freight trains. The conversation above comes from *Rolling Nowhere* (Penguin, 1982), the book Ted wrote about his year on the rails.

Ted eventually became a successful magazine writer, and he has written two books since *Rolling Nowhere*. Never, however, did he envision a career evolving directly from his time off. "I never imagined when I set off that I might write a book. Certainly, I'd never met anyone except some professors who had written a book. I think I hadn't been brought up to be that ambitious," he recalled.

Ted grew up in Denver, where as a white student he found himself bused across town to a black high school the city was attempting to integrate. "Amherst was socially homogeneous, which I wasn't used to. And performance standards were very high. All of it was a bit jarring.

"It was the beginning of my sophomore year when I started feeling restless, thinking that there must be more to life than this.

"I was being asked to choose my major, which would presumably influence my choice of career, but I'd really done nothing my whole life except go to school. How, if school is your main experience in the world, are you supposed to know what you want to do in the world after school?

"For all the advantages Amherst had, and the ivory tower has many, a disadvantage can be the lack of exposure to other people and other places. So I didn't feel like I was leaving education when I left Amherst, I felt that I was leaving to broaden my education."

Ted left college to live in Dallas for a year as a VISTA (Volunteers in Service to America) worker. "A lot of my friends were planning junior years abroad, and I considered that, but I had always been struck by how many of my friends knew more about Europe than about the United States. I thought I could spend junior year at home, if you will, and just not get credit for it.

"We were doing community organizing to empower the lower-income people there. That was the line, and it was mostly true." Ted worked in a Dallas neighborhood, and his duties included organizing tenants, running crime-prevention programs, and working with teens. VISTA paid just enough to sustain the modest standard of living he had been accustomed to as a student. Ted returned to Amherst a more focused student, and a more focused person. "After fifteen months, I was ready to go back. I had a better idea of what I wanted, and socially, I had a better idea of who I was and where I fit in, of what mattered and what didn't. I declared an anthropology major, and I moved off-campus. My grades, which had been so-so, started a steady climb after I returned."

As Ted read more anthropology, however, the wanderlust began to nip at his heels once more. Ever since he was a child, he had been fascinated by railroad hoboes. Slowly, he began to imagine what it might be like to study them himself.

After reading a few ancient books on hobo life and a smattering of magazine and newspaper articles from the previous ten years, Ted said it became clear that no one had done much recent anthropological fieldwork on hoboes. The lack of work, he later wrote in his thesis on railroad hoboes, almost made it seem as if the hobo way of life had died out sometime during the middle of the century.

But Ted had a hunch that hoboes were still around. "I didn't think they were dying off, and I justified the sort of romantic idea of riding the rails as a worthwhile activity because anthropology made me think that I wouldn't just be riding for fun and adventure. I'd be riding to learn and observe and maybe later to bear witness in some way to what I had seen and heard."

Ted's suggestion that he might bear witness to hobo culture in the form of an undergraduate honors thesis struck his professors as somewhat mad. While they didn't rule it out, they generally discouraged Ted with the observation that it was a highly dangerous thing to do. "One professor asked whether I had considered the possibility of homosexual rape out there," he said.

"VISTA didn't seem to worry my parents too much, but this did. They had never stopped me from doing anything since I was fifteen, but my mother was worried about my safety. My father, on the other hand, seemed to have a suspicion that this was an elaborate way of goofing off. Some of my friends were also skeptical. 'Why would hoboes want to talk to a guy like you?' they asked me.

"But in a way that sort of discouragement was a source of inspiration. You just get to the point where you want to show them that you *can* make it happen."

So that fall Ted avoided the crowds of back-to-school shoppers at the mall and went to the Salvation Army store instead.

"How did tramps look? Taking a calculated guess, I outfitted myself with secondhand clothing, let my hair grow long, grew a beard, and got dirty," he wrote in his thesis. "I carried a small used shoulder bag (for my notes, tape recorder, and other valuables) and a bedroll.

"Figuring the best place to meet tramps was near trains, and that an understanding of trains was necessary to living their life, I got on the rails as soon as possible.

"It was not easy. Unfamiliar with the workings of railroad yards, of the freedom the tramp may have in them and the etiquette he must observe, it took me two days after meeting that first tramp to 'catch out' of St. Louis for Kansas City, and two more days to actually arrive there."

Though Ted quickly got better at hopping freights, trying to relate to the tramps that he met along the way was never easy. While he did all the same things they did, sleeping in shelters, exploiting the welfare system, and selling his blood, the line between Ted Conover and the identity he created for himself was admittedly somewhat fuzzy.

"It was an intense experiment in self-identity," he recalled. "I think anytime you willingly relocate yourself and plop yourself down in a different cultural milieu, you're going to have that.

"I wasn't always free to tell people who I was or where I came from. Sometimes it put me in peril, so I would keep things to myself that might have been better spoken about for my own peace of mind.

"It was incredibly important to me to be accepted by these people who were not like me, so I would hide parts of myself in order to be accepted by them. I think most anthropologists do this. In fact, I think many people who are members of a minority have to do it, too, and it works on all kinds of different levels."

While passing through his hometown for the first time, Ted was arrested on a bridge. The President of the United States was in town, and the Denver police had been told not to allow any derelicts on the bridge. Ted was charged with disobeying the order of a police officer: "Hurry up, asshole!" to be exact.

"Man, I thought, would I love to tell him a thing or two," Ted wrote in *Rolling Nowhere.* "The name of my college would be a good place to start . . . and then I might just mention that my dad headed up a big law firm downtown—ever heard of it? No? Well, you're gonna, you bastard. Just as soon as I get to a telephone, somebody's head's gonna roll."

But then he stopped himself. "It would be too easy. Revenge would be sweet, but it would prove nothing. I would show only that I wasn't what I appeared to be. That was the opposite of my objective: to let people believe I was somebody else and see how I was treated, see what life was like from the other side. It had gotten a bit tough, and I was ready to give up." So, instead of calling his father, Ted spent the night in jail.

The reward for his perseverance came midway through his journey, as he approached a man dismantling a boxcar for firewood on the outskirts of a small town.

> *"Hey," the man asked. "You a tramp?"*
>
> *"What?"*
>
> *"I said, 'Are you a tramp?' "*
>
> *Few questions could have caught me so off-guard . . . This struck right at the heart of the matter.*
>
> *"Yeah," I answered, too defensively. "I guess I am." I was amazed at how close the words came to ringing true. In part because my desire was so strong, the jungles were becoming my home. For weeks I had been concerned with appearances . . . When tramps looked at me, would they see themselves . . . But now I saw that I had neglected what was going on inside. Sloughing off that feeling of being an outsider . . . was essential to achieving the ease of mind and manners that would make tramps see me as one of them. "Yeah, I guess I am," I had said, and it struck me that, to a degree, saying it had made it so.*

As his time on the rails wore on, however, Ted also felt the need to differentiate himself from the tramps. "At night I would steal away to brush my teeth, just to remind myself that I had teeth and I planned to keep them, whereas a lot of the hoboes didn't have them anymore."

He also called his friends collect, partly to remind himself that there were people who would pay to talk to him.

Those phone calls, however, were sometimes a source of anxiety. As Ted explained in his book, near the end of his trip, he called his college roommate to voice some of his frustrations.

Trying to be helpful, his roommate told him to look on the bright side: Ted could rest easy now, knowing that if anything ever went really wrong, he could still get by as a tramp.

> *The remark, only partly serious, had been intended as a comfort, but it had entirely the opposite effect. Hearing someone who knew me propose trampdom as a conceivable destiny for me was utterly depressing . . . In a complete turnabout from my earlier concerns, I wanted a guarantee that, while I could get close to tramps, I could never really become one . . . I wanted someone I knew to say that going native sounded more absurd to them than it did to me right now.*

It was at that point that Ted realized it was time to start winding his way back to Denver. His homecoming was to be a surprise. He did not tell his family when he would be arriving, in the hope that they might not recognize him when he finally rang the doorbell.

And they didn't. "Some things can probably be imagined without too many details. Double takes are such a movie cliché, but it was a true classic. My sister came to the door and I asked for Mrs. Conover. She said to wait just a minute, but a few seconds later she turned around and whispered, 'Ted?' It was wonderful."

Ted returned to Amherst that winter with 450 pages of notes and observations. Safe and sound, he was welcomed with open arms by the professors in the Anthropology Department, who helped him mold his research on the American hobo into a thesis which won him the highest possible honors.

Reintegrating into life at Amherst was not as difficult as Ted anticipated. "I was a bit nervous about returning to college, because there's a hobo part of me that likes the idea of freedom from schedules and deadlines, and college is all about schedules and deadlines," he said.

"Because I was working on my own so much that last semester, school wasn't as bad as I thought it would be. I was an independent scholar, essentially an interdisciplinary hobo major. When hoboes became my thesis, I could talk about my experiences as well as my work when we sat around the tables in the dining hall. So it wasn't ultimately as alienating as it might have been."

Ted wrote an article about his experiences on the rails for the Amherst alumni magazine that spring. A few days after it came out, he was interviewed by an Associated Press reporter who had seen his story. In the remarkable sequence of events that followed, the AP story went out over the national wires and Ted received interview requests from the *Today* show, *Good Morning America*, and National Public Radio. "It was such a riot—so surreal," he said.

Luckily, the calls didn't start coming in until a few days after he had finished his thesis. Looking back on what he had written, however, Ted realized that there was another story lurking between the lines of his ethnography—his own.

While he was in New York appearing on the *Today* show, Ted met with a literary agent who happened to have grown up near one of the largest railroad yards in the country. Within three weeks, the agent had sold Ted's book proposal for *Rolling Nowhere*.

"I had to call the *Indianapolis Star*, because I was supposed to work for them that summer, to tell them that I might need to take a few long weekends to meet with an editor in New York," he recalled. "And they just said no, if you feel like you're going to need that many days, you should let someone more deserving have the internship.

"I had never walked away from a job before, but at that point I did. By then, I had this odd new job, which is what I still do, writing for myself. I'm a self-employed writer."

It's been well over ten years now since Ted last lived on the rails, but he said that some of the lessons he learned as a hobo have stuck.

"In the best of all possible worlds, you're not just a kid and then an adult," he explained. "Growing up is not something that ends when you leave college. On the rails, I came to understand identity as a mutable thing. I have a strong sense of who I am, but I also know that that sense changes, and I have almost come to expect to see it change.

"Profound change is possible at any point in your life, perhaps even desirable. If you're going to *live*, in italics, at the highest pitch possible, you have to be ready to try something completely different.

"I hope my experience isn't isolated. I think that one of the greatest things about the extended adolescence in this country is that, with luck, you can take some chances, you can do something that wasn't in the plans for you.

"Who knows? It could be a waste of time, but it could be something you'll always remember. For me, it totally shifted the direction of my life, and I think what a huge mistake it would have been not to take those chances."

MILES GILLIOM

Roswell, Georgia

BROWN UNIVERSITY '94

As a teenager growing up in a house filled with four siblings and two cousins, Miles Gilliom often felt the need for a quiet hike alone in the woods behind his house. But his love for the outdoors had been cultivated long before his house got so crowded.

"My parents have always been interested in the outdoors, and we did a fair amount of camping when I was little. I also went to a day camp, and once a summer we would take an overnight trip. The counselors there displayed a real reverence for the woods, and that was something that I wanted to emulate."

Although Miles occasionally brought his mom along on his treks through the woods, he usually went by himself. "I think that's always been my nature. Given the choice to be in a large group setting or on my own, I would often take the latter."

However, Miles made an exception for his dog, Merlin, who was always up for a walk. The dog was one thing that didn't get shared in the Gilliom house; Miles's father, who worked in marketing for IBM at the time, and his mother, a counselor in private practice, bought him the dog for his four-teenth birthday.

Miles chose to attend Brown University. "Suddenly I was at a school where people had parents who were CEOs of corporations and doctors and lawyers. I guess I was feeling like a lot of people had had a lot more exposure than I had to the world," he said.

"I think I was so excited about the prospect of going to Brown that I didn't spend enough time thinking about what I might find when I got there. And I immediately found myself overloaded with coursework and not really knowing how to make decisions in terms of charting my academic future."

Miles first began to consider time off as his freshman year concluded. "Freshman year was really up and down. I was beginning to think that one of the things that I wanted to do was to step back from the pace my life was taking and just reassess a bit."

Miles elected to return for his sophomore year, but a painful ending to a romantic relationship and a particularly difficult year as a dorm counselor convinced him that his initial hunch had been correct.

He considered enrolling in an organized trek/academic semester in Nepal through the School for International Training, but he ultimately decided against it. "I eventually decided that I was more interested in doing something on my own, having some time where I would really be making my own choices. I think I felt I had just been responding for a long time, especially at school."

During his sophomore year, Miles and a few friends had spent three days hiking the Appalachian Trail, a continuous path that runs from Maine to Georgia. After that trip, Miles was convinced that taking a longer solo trek down the trail would be the best way to spend a semester away from Brown. And, of course, Merlin would come along.

Miles had camped with his parents when he was younger and been on plenty of day hikes, but his knowledge of how to prepare for a mega-journey was limited. "There was just a low sort of underlying feeling of anxiety about the whole thing—not having any idea what it would be like to be in a tent fifty miles from the nearest town. Putting energy into making arrangements was a big way of allaying the anxiety aroused by taking on a new way of life, and I think I gained so much from just deciding to throw myself into it. Whatever you do, do it with gusto," he said.

"There is a whole community of people who have hiked the AT, people who are really willing to talk about their experiences, and I think they were probably the best resources. I met one person who worked in an outdoors store who had taken time off and spent three months on the AT. He gave me a lot of advice in terms of what kind of weather to expect, what kind of gear would be best, how to feed myself, and how much I could expect to spend." Miles also called the Appalachian Mountain Club, which has a wealth of resources for people planning to hike the trail.

As for equipment, Miles was basically starting from scratch. He needed boots, a tent, a camping stove, a sleeping bag, and a golden retriever–sized knapsack. "I bought the best equipment I could find. After equipment costs and paying for the plane ticket up to Maine, I ended up spending about a dollar a mile for my 700-mile trip," which is about average, he said.

Miles's college scholarship from IBM entitled him to a summer job there, so he signed on for a well-paying post to pay off his equipment debts. "I just decided that earning lots of money was going to be the main focus of the summer," he said.

When he was not on the job or playing with his band, the Porchhonkys, Miles was training for his expedition. "I went on a couple of camping trips to really get acquainted with my gear. I did a fair amount of running and some training hikes, where I would load my pack with forty pounds of books and just walk around the woods for three to four hours," he recalled.

As his departure date got closer, Miles began to think about what he wanted to accomplish in the seventy-five days he planned to spend on the trail. As he explained it, however, he believed that "goals" might be more of an obstacle than a focus. "I wanted to shift my emphasis from the 'goal' to the process and to make the process become the goal. Leaving things open, so that I would be closed to nothing. And I think that was enforced by what I found in living that way—that things could be more wonderful than I ever planned them to be."

Before Miles left, a friend gave him a journal. "There were so many things that lent themselves to journal writing. The experiences were so new and rich that it was very easy to write," he said.

Miles and Merlin arrived in Maine in mid-September, armed only with a sign saying, "Two hikers going to Appalachian Trail," which was a good hundred miles away from the airport. A couple picked them up almost immediately and drove thirty miles out of their way to drop the campers at the beginning of the trail.

Miles's decisions to start in September and hike from the north to the south were slightly out of the ordinary. Most people start in March in the south and finish early in the fall. Miles knew he wouldn't be hiking the entire trail, and since he started in September, he needed to hike away from the cold weather.

"The first stretch of trail is called the hundred-mile wilderness. It's by far the most isolated part of trail. It really was a trial by fire. There are no chances to resupply, so I was carrying a week's worth of my own food and of Merlin's food."

AT hikers tend to be a food-preoccupied bunch, and Miles was no exception. He had shopped for most of his food before he left Georgia and left it packed in boxes for his parents to ship to post offices along his intended route. He would receive a two-week-supply box from home, put half the food in his pack, then send the other half to a post office farther south, where he could pick it up a week later.

"Basically, you can't eat enough when you're hiking, so the stops on the trail are really essential. Walking fifteen to twenty miles a day with a full pack, you burn the same amount of calories as you would running two full marathons. I'd try to find a Shoney's or some other all-you-can-eat restaurant and just settle down and chow to get my calories back up. I'd also buy food along the way, good packable stuff like peanut butter and candy bars."

For Merlin, eating was also something of a ritual. "I had Science Diet dog food, really high-performance stuff for him. But after the first ten days, it was clear that he wasn't getting enough. I started buying extra ramen noodles and mixed it in with his food. It would make this nice stew, which he just loved. He was so funny. He'd wait for it to cool, then pick up the whole bowl in his mouth and carry it off into the woods out of sight. I'd hear this chomping sound and then he would come back about ten minutes later with a fat belly. Then he'd plop right down and sleep for about fourteen hours.

"He really was a great companion. I think his tolerance level was pretty similar to mine. I wouldn't always pay such close attention to how I was feeling or whether or not it would be good to stop and rest or get some food in my body. So, if he was looking pretty miserable, I'd stop and realize I wasn't feeling so great myself."

Miles and Merlin tended to set their clocks by the sun. "We would get into camp about an hour before the sun went down to set up and cook dinner. Some nights, we'd be asleep by seven and we wouldn't wake up until six the next morning," he said. "We tended to camp out if the weather was nice, and if it looked like rain we'd shoot for a shelter." The Appalachian Mountain Club maintains many shelters on the trail.

"I was really happy out there. The day was pretty simple. I'd spend my time walking or looking at the map or reading or sleeping. I thought a lot about my connections at Brown and my place at Brown. I thought about my whole life. I tried to go back to my earliest memories and then through elementary school and high school. I thought about my dreams. There was also a lot of time when I was just looking around at the places I was passing through. I realized that I had never had that kind of control before, ever, over my own day."

Occasionally, however, Miles found his path blocked. "We had reached the summit of a mountain and we heard something coming our way. Merlin froze, and there was a huge bull moose with a monster set of antlers about twenty feet ahead. Merlin barged past me to show the moose who's boss, and he almost got out a bark when it bared its teeth and charged right at us. I got into a stand of trees and Merlin just got the heck out."

Most of Miles's trail encounters were a bit less harrowing. All sorts of characters are out hiking the trail at any given time, but one of his favorites was a man named Vagabond Lou. "He's about seventy now, and I think he's hiked the AT four or five times. He's been struck by lightning three times and been body-searched by a full-grown bear. A pretty crazy old man, an incredible person."

As a general rule, however, Miles and Merlin hiked alone. One night Miles wrote in his journal:

I think this is the first day in my entire life where I haven't seen another human being. It is a quiet way to live and filled with possibilities. There is no self-consciousness in being alone, but much consciousness. Will I be able to remember that when I get back into the world of other people? God, I hope so.

Miles's parents had been supportive all along, and their only request was that he call home every so often. "It was interesting when I called home, the difficulty of going from acting as an individual to being part of a family. I'd feel myself slipping back into one of many—one of nine—modes and felt frustrated trying to express what I was feeling and experiencing. They were supportive, but I think they had no idea what it was like."

Miles finally got the chance to share his experiences when his dad joined him for a weekend on the trail. Miles had found a ride from Vermont to Virginia with a woman he had met on the trail. His dad met him a week later for a few days of hiking and dropped him and Merlin off in North Carolina to hike the rest of the trail on their own. They finished just before Thanksgiving, and Miles returned to Brown in January.

By the time Miles made it back to Rhode Island, he was flat broke. "I had been able to save a lot of money from my summer job but I spent it all. It was a pretty lean semester. That's something to think about. I spent so much time focusing on paying for my time away that I didn't think too much about what would come after.

"I think that some of the jubilation of the trip faded with time. Since then, it has helped to go back to the journal. I was happy to find out that, upon returning, I really could continue to live deliberately to a certain extent. Obviously, I had a lot of things I had to do—writing papers and taking tests—but I could make each class much more personal.

"The choice to take time off and the way you fill the time is such a personal one. I was really lucky to stumble into what was ideal for me. Just having my own time, my own space, was really what I needed."

> *It was a slow sad walk down the mountain. And a cold hungry one too. But these woods are here, waiting for our return. So much we learned and experienced among the trees and the mountains of Appalachia over the last few months. We will be back for sure. What lies in the future, we don't know, but we will find out.*
>
> > *Signed,*
> > *Miles and Merlin,*
> > *mountain explorers extraordinaire*

HILLARY ZAZOVE

Skokie, Illinois
UNIVERSITY OF MONTANA '96

The best thing about high school for Hillary Zazove was that it ended.

"I can honestly say I did not really learn anything in high school," she said. "I'm serious. I would testify to that. I think I came out of there dumber."

Attendance was not a priority. "I was barely attending school," she said. "If they said you can only miss ninety-two days, I would miss ninety-two days. I marked the days in my calendar." Going to college was also not a major concern. "I don't even know if the school had a college counselor," she said.

Certain that she wanted to be away from the classroom, but unsure of what to do, Hillary began to explore various options. She also wrestled with the concerns of her parents, who viewed not being in school as a risky proposition. "My dad didn't want to have to worry about me," she said.

During her final year at Niles North High School in Illinois, a family friend took an interest in her. "Mr. Baxter gave me a brochure about NOLS, the National Outdoor Leadership School. NOLS runs outdoor education and leadership training programs around the world. The thought of him giving me that brochure and having enough confidence in me to think that I should take it home and show my folks totally helped my self-esteem."

Hillary applied to NOLS's Fall Semester in the Rockies, one of their longer, more challenging, and more expensive courses. She was required to write an application essay and submit some financial documents to qualify for their scholarship program.

"It cost a lot," she said. "I paid for part of it, I got $2,000 deferred to pay off as a loan, and NOLS gave me $2,500 in scholarship money. My parents are both Chicago public school teachers, and they weren't making enough money to justify spending $6,000 on just one semester."

After graduating from high school in 1989, Hillary lived at home and got a job working at a health club. Her goal was to make money until she began the NOLS trip in September of 1990. "My parents knew that I was being responsible and that I was trying to do something that was going to be positive for me."

The job meshed well with her growing passion for athletics. "To help get in shape for my trip, I was running all the time and lifting weights. I felt really good about myself."

Meanwhile, reports from her friends who had gone off to college did not make Hillary feel that she was missing much. "They were like 'Oh, it's so cool. There's all these cute guys, everyone totally parties, I live in these dorms, the campus is really pretty and the food sucks.' "

NOLS sent Hillary extensive information about how to prepare for the trip. They made packing suggestions, encouraged participants to exercise as much as possible, and included reading material about the areas where the group would be traveling.

Instead of spending lots of money on new camping gear, Hillary simply used the equipment which NOLS issues free to anyone who needs it. "You don't have to buy any of it, which makes the trip much more affordable," she said.

The Fall Semester in the Rockies provides students with a comprehensive introduction to technical outdoor skills. Hillary's trip included a mountain section, canyon hiking, winter skiing, caving, and rock climbing. The group learned basic wilderness living skills such as cooking, stove use and repair, map reading, route finding, and first aid. They then progressed to a study of plant and animal identification, geology, prehistoric Indian cultures, and the natural history of the area.

"We lived outdoors, prepared our own meals, and took care of ourselves," Hillary recalled. NOLS also emphasizes minimum-impact camping. Students are encouraged to leave no trace of their presence. The seventeen students in her group traveled in small groups of four to six to minimize their impact on the environment.

"We hiked seven to ten miles a day carrying backpacks that weighed over sixty-five pounds," she said. Initially, the groups included an instructor, but they later traveled alone.

Hillary was also able to do a "solo," spend a day and a night alone in the wilderness. Members of her group who chose to do so were also able to go through the student-led expedition without food. The fasting section was designed to increase participants' confidence about their ability to survive if they find themselves unexpectedly stranded someday.

"We hiked through the canyon country of the Colorado Plateau in southern Utah. We came up over the top of a cliff and a huge expanse of land spread out below us. Our group had found a place called the Valley of the Gods. Huge mesas twenty miles apart rose up in incredible shapes and colors everywhere."

Each participant was required to keep a journal. Hillary wrote down what she was learning about plant and animal identification, the Anasazi culture, and the area's ecosystems. She also studied for and successfully passed NOLS's Wilderness First Aid course; she was one of the few people on the trip to do so.

In the winter section of the course, the group learned the basics of snow camping, skiing, avalanche safety, snow physics, cold-weather physiology, and winter ecology. "Winter section was really cold but it was fun. We built igloos and read Jack London stories by our lanterns at night."

Hillary believes that she came back from NOLS a changed person. "It wasn't until I got home that I realized what a big thing that had been for me. I knew I could basically learn anything if given the right opportunity.

"In high school, one of the reasons I didn't learn anything was that I kind of thought I was dumb. Maybe that's why I never even thought about college. I didn't think I had the potential to go to college and be successful."

Going on a NOLS trip gave Hillary an opportunity to test her abilities in a new environment. "I was with all these people who were taking time off from college. Many of them had been enrolled for a year or two, were doing NOLS, and then going back. I realized that I was at their level. I was capable of handling myself in very diverse situations. Challenging, technical situations, taking tests, learning wilderness first aid."

NOLS helped Hillary overcome the distaste for learning she had developed during an unrewarding high school career. "It was hands-on learning," she said. "It was not like sitting in a classroom with a teacher who you probably thought just went home and watched TV at night.

"It's hard to want to learn from someone you don't respect. I respected the NOLS instructors and wanted to hear what they had to say."

After successfully completing the NOLS course, Hillary was accepted at the University of Montana. She found it easy to incorporate what she had learned during her NOLS trip into her new college life.

"I started an outdoors/camping/skiing group in the dorm to take advantage of what I had learned on my trip. I also became interested in endurance running and endurance cycling. And I started doing triathalons."

Hillary elected to pursue a communications major, and has considered becoming a social worker. "I feel there are so many people out there who genuinely are not having their needs met. Women who are trying to get off welfare, or elderly people stuck in rest homes, for example. They're feeling unsatisfied, unfulfilled, frustrated, fed up, and angry. I want to be able to talk to them and try to help them meet their needs.

"NOLS gave me a huge confidence boost about school. I hung out with the healthy crowd, not with a bunch of partiers. We would do our homework. I wouldn't miss any classes. I would sit, listen, and take notes. I was a sponge for information. I was in really great physical and mental shape. I didn't resent going to class. It was my choice to be there."

ABBEY MARBLE

Lake Oswego, Oregon

BROWN UNIVERSITY '93

When Abbey Marble briefly considered taking time off after finishing high school in Lake Oswego, a suburb of Portland, Oregon, she found herself swimming upstream. "Everybody around me was taking the SAT, writing essays, applying to colleges, going through interviews—all the stuff that I dreaded," she said.

"I wondered what it would feel like to be stuck in Portland living at home when all my friends went off to college. I have always gotten along well with my parents, but it would have been hard to be as independent as I felt I needed to be if I was still living at home. The most immediate way to become more independent was to go to college."

Abbey began at Brown University in the fall of 1989. "The amount of activities in college was overwhelming. I went to meetings for this and meetings for that. I wrote an article here and did an illustration there."

By the time she made it to the summer after her sophomore year, Abbey yearned for a break to allow her to form a better idea of what she wanted to be getting out of Brown. She started tossing around ideas with Matt, a friend from high school, and together they resolved to ride their bikes across America.

"I spent the rest of the summer working a seven-hour morning shift in a coffeeshop. After work, I biked to get in shape."

The trip was not expensive. "People absolutely can do an expedition like this. It's totally affordable. During the trip itself, we basically only spent money on food, which amounted to roughly $10 a day. As for what we spent on equipment before we left, our philosophy was less is more and cheaper is better.

"We started out with a two-person tent, sleeping bags, rain gear, a bike-repair kit, and a stove named Oscar because it was so grouchy. We packed John Steinbeck's *Travels with Charlie* and kept trading books with people as we went along."

By midtrip, Abbey was in phenomenal shape. "We averaged about seventy miles a day, with a few hundred-mile days thrown in."

The ride gave her lots of time to think. "If you want a chance to reflect about your life, get on a bike and ride for eight hours every day. Thirty percent of the time, I was thinking, 'Oh my God, I'm so tired,' or 'My knee hurts,' but that's to be expected.

"The West Coast and the Midwest were one big outdoor adventure. The scenery was monumentally beautiful. As we approached the East Coast, it became more of an experience of meeting people."

Abbey came up with ingenious ways to encourage strangers to lend her and Matt a helping hand. "We stayed with a lot of strangers that we met on the road. We would bike up to people and ask if they knew if there was a park somewhere in town where we could camp out. Usually, when you ask somebody that, they let you camp in their yard, at least. Sometimes they even let you have a shower.

"Being on a bike makes a big difference. People are immediately interested in you and where you're from and what you're doing. And you don't look threatening when you're on a bicycle."

The biking duo sometimes found help in unexpected places. "We went into a doughnut shop and someone said, 'Oh, you're on a bike trip? Do you want to be on the radio?'

"So we went on the radio and talked about our trip for a little bit. We mentioned that we hoped to make it to Warsaw, Missouri, that night. Just as we were getting off the air, someone called the station and said, 'We live in Warsaw. Come and stay with us if you make it here.' It was great."

When they made it to Warsaw, Abbey said she was reminded of how unusual her adventure seemed to some people. "The woman we stayed with was shocked that I had the freedom to do this. On her wall, she had her high school graduation certificate, a portrait of her senior prom, and her wedding photo. I looked closer at her high school diploma. She had graduated the year after me. And they were trying to have children."

Abbey said most people assumed she and Matt were married. Others were puzzled as to why she had chosen to bike such a long way. "Lots of people asked me, 'Your parents let you do this?'

"My only fear was not knowing ahead of time where I was going to sleep, but I was continually surprised by how easy it was. We once knocked on someone's door and asked if we could camp on their lawn. They said sure, and then insisted on taking us out to dinner that night and breakfast the next morning."

Exhaustion began to set in as the final leg of the trip to Washington, D.C., approached. "The roads were narrower and there was more traffic the farther east we got, and more people and situations that made me nervous sleeping at night."

Getting off her bike and onto the nine-to-five schedule back home was difficult. "It just sucked. I flew home shortly before Christmas and entered the retail hell of the pre-Christmas season. I felt like I had never really processed the trip at all."

When she returned to Brown, Abbey said she was "unexpectedly picking and choosing what was important to me without consciously trying to do so.

"Everyone should be required to attend one semester of college and then take a year off. That way, they would know about all the opportunities they were coming back to and could focus on choosing the ones they wanted to pursue."

PART FIVE

Getting Back on Track

Most of the people we talked to who looked back on their time off with ambivalence had one thing in common: they left school without establishing a plan for themselves. Instead of working toward a goal, many of them were running from a problem. Their reasoning was: "Well, I'll get away from something that is bad, and then once I do, a successful year will materialize out of the blue." The fact is that it just doesn't work that way. If you are going to take time off, you must put every effort into setting goals and formulating a plan to achieve them.

Other students needed to leave school because the plan they had formulated was not working out. Instead of wasting one of their eight semesters while struggling with a problem, some students left school simply to get things under control, and **then** they came back to school.

DANIELLE STEPHENS

Seattle, Washington

UNIVERSITY OF WASHINGTON '97

It wasn't until Danielle Stephens had to work to dig herself out from underneath a whopping $10,000 credit-card debt that she realized how fortunate she was to have been raised by a great mother.

"I was adopted at birth and my mom did what she could to get by. When she was divorced, she worked hard to make sure we never had to go on welfare. My work ethic totally comes from her. If your legs work and your arms work, get out there. Work hard, be honest, and do your best."

Danielle's troubles with credit cards began shortly after she graduated from high school in Seattle in 1987. When she told her family she wanted to go on to a community college, not everyone thought it was the right thing to do. "My grandparents worked on farms back in North Dakota. Their mentality was 'School is not a necessity. You go and work on the farm because that's where the help is most needed. A high school education or a college diploma isn't going to milk the cow.' "

Danielle went ahead and enrolled at Green River Community College in Auburn, Washington. Community college was more affordable than a four-year college and also gave Danielle a chance to improve her study skills, which she feared were not up to university standards. Her goal was to get a two-year Associate of Arts degree and fulfill the general requirements necessary for enrollment at the University of Washington.

She also had a future occupation in mind. "I would be in heaven if I could work for Nike and get free tennis shoes and work for Toyota and get free cars. Those are my two passions in life, shoes and cars. Things that get me where I want to go, you know what I'm saying?"

Trouble began for Danielle when she indulged her passion for Nikes and Toyotas before she was an employee of either company. Danielle had a part-time job while she was attending the community college, but she was not earning enough money to make ends meet.

"I was not keeping track of my money," she explained. "I had two Visas, a MasterCard, a Discover Card, an American Express, a Nordstrom's, a Texaco, a telephone calling card, you name it. You know that joke about the guy who whips out his wallet with the pictures of all his kids and it keeps unrolling forever? I was packing twenty pounds of plastic in my wallet.

"I used my credit cards to get cash advances from automatic teller machines. I must have thought money grew on trees, because I was spending it like it did."

She had bought a Toyota and was having a hard time making the payments. "I was paying 440 bucks a month for this car and reality started to hit. I was already at a disadvantage because of my underdeveloped study skills, and I realized I needed to work less hours and study more. Which meant I'd be making less money, and if I was making less money, that probably meant I couldn't keep the car."

Danielle's credit cards were so maxed out that she couldn't use them anymore. Most credit card companies require cardholders to make minimum monthly payments on their debt. They also charge cardholders for the debt they carry over from one month to the next, a charge sometimes levied at interest rates of 18 percent or higher. Her minimum monthly payments were going toward paying off the interest she had been charged. She was not even making a dent in the $10,000 principal.

"I was in way over my head. I had completely overdone it and I had no idea what to do. My mental stability was in jeopardy because I was constantly worried about how I was going to pay for everything."

To regain control of her finances, she sought assistance at a nonprofit budget and credit counseling organization. The organization took over all her outstanding debt and consolidated it into one large loan that she could pay back in regular monthly installments at a lower interest rate. They also took away all her credit cards.

"They made me sit down with them and list all my expenses. Rent, food, everything. They asked me to figure out the next time I was going to need underwear. They wanted me to save in advance, to make a budget and put money into a savings account. That way, six months from now, when I needed to buy new underwear, I would have the money.

"It seemed foolish to me, but to them it was a critical piece of altering the life-style. They made me take a long hard look at where I was blowing my cash."

The organization put Danielle on a four-year program to

pay off her debt. She was required to pay them $300 each month by money order. The organization then paid her bills, dispensing an agreed-upon amount to her creditors. Credit-counseling agencies usually try to convince the credit-card companies to reduce or altogether eliminate interest charges, which they were able to do in Danielle's case.

Danielle was especially glad that she no longer had to field calls from an army of bill collectors. She compared gaining control over her finances to someone who goes on a diet and learns to control his or her eating habits. "When your doctor says you need to go on a diet, if you don't reduce the amount that you eat, your daily calories, then you're going to get fatter. Well, my daily calories were dollars and my weight was my debt.

"You know how some dietitians ask people what kind of mood they were in when they were eating? They asked me, 'What kind of mood were you in when you spent that money?' And I realized that whenever I was depressed or angry, the first thing I would do was charge. I was a fat pig in debt!"

When Danielle thinks back on all the things she learned in high school, she wonders why she wasn't required to take Balancing Your Checkbook 101. "I went through so much financial trauma because no one bothered to show me how to manage money," she said.

As part of her struggle to regain control over her finances, Danielle left school and went to work full-time. She was able to get a job as a cashier at Costco, a store similar to Wal-Mart, in 1990. "I started making the big bucks, $8 an hour. I've been there for the past five years," she said.

After spending two years working full-time, Danielle was able to pay off nearly all her original debt. At that time, she considered going back to school again.

Meeting her birth mom for the first time in 1991 provided Danielle with the final inspiration she needed. "She didn't come right out and say, 'Get your butt in school,' " Danielle remembered. "She just asked me if I was happy, if the people around me were satisfied, and if I thought I could be working there as a cashier ten years from now and still be happy.

"I kept telling myself, 'Okay, I'm going to pay the bills off and then I'll go to school.' I was never able to completely pay off all my debt, so I decided it made more sense to go ahead and get my degree.

"If I could tell young people one thing, I would tell them to go to school and get their education. And to borrow the money if they need to. An education is something that no one can take away from you. It is yours and yours exclusively, and it has a value."

In 1992, Danielle returned to school part-time at Green River Community College, while continuing to work at Costco. Going to school while holding down a job has sometimes been difficult.

"At Costco, they came to rely on me. They would call at four in the morning and say, 'Hi, we need you, can you be here in five minutes? Someone called in sick.' I lived nearby and would get there in a heartbeat.

"Meanwhile, I would have a paper due. Yet I was at work because, well, you kind of like to eat and you might want to pay the rent, just maybe, and you learn that sometimes school loses out.

"Sometimes my finances are a barricade between me and being successful in school. Otherwise, I could be completely relentless in the pursuit of my goals.

"Based on the experiences I've had, I can go to work and turn off school while I'm there. But when I come home, I still haven't really figured out how to turn school on. If we lived in a perfect world, it wouldn't be necessary to fight for an education. It would be provided for somehow."

Danielle graduated with her A.A. degree in the winter of 1994, posting a 4.0 GPA her last quarter there. She then enrolled directly into the University of Washington. She credits her community-college experience with giving her the tools and the motivation necessary to continue with her education.

"A lot of people get stuck in a pattern of failure because they have dropped out of school at some point in their lives and they base their future expectations on that one past experience. 'Look what happened last time I went. It didn't work for me.' Community college helped me build a desire to succeed."

Danielle is currently a political-science major at the University of Washington and has considered transferring some of what she has learned into a career in politics. "What's being done with our tax dollars? Government spending today is like someone calling me up and saying, 'Hey, I spent all my money. Can I borrow some of yours?' No, you can't, because I need it to live. I can't even get the government to give me a Pell grant, because I am supposedly making so much money as a cashier. Meanwhile, I pay my taxes and am eating a lot of top ramen soup."

Sometimes Danielle finds herself wishing she had not been forced to grow up so quickly. "As an eighteen-year-old you have the world by the tail and everything is going for you," she said. "You've got youth on your side. Sometimes I want to be eighteen again. No responsibilities, no debts. I want to know what it's like to be able to pick up my backpack and my camp stove and a sleeping bag and just go. 'I'm out of here. Tell Nordstrom's if they call that I'll pay them in a few months when I get back.'

"Sometimes I get mad at those people whose parents hand them $500 a month. They can go out and drink beer or do whatever they want. And then I think, 'You know what, I am so much better off than they are, because I *know*. Reality bites, man. You've got to pay the rent.' "

ERIK BRISSON

Providence, Rhode Island

MASSACHUSETTS INSTITUTE OF TECHNOLOGY '75

Computers at Boston University are linked by a multimillion-dollar network, the center of which sits behind double security doors on a quiet street just off the campus's main drag.

Erik Brisson manages all the graphics programming there, writing code and teaching faculty and students to manipulate it in precise ways.

Though the intricate minutia of the programmer's life often govern Erik's day-to-day existence, he was not always such a detail man. As an undergraduate at MIT, he discovered first-hand what happens to a "system" that lacks an appropriate programmed "plan."

Erik lived in Alabama until he was eight years old and then his parents, who were art professors, moved the family to Rhode Island. "As I was growing up, college was pretty much part of life for our family. But my parents also had a lot of time off. They had their summers, and their schedules were flexible," he recalled.

Erik attended public schools in Rhode Island, and almost immediately it became clear that his artistic genes were recessive. "The earliest thing I can remember was being six or seven and wanting to be a herpetologist, because I really loved snakes. I was good at math and science in a way that my parents just weren't. I could excel at that and rebel against the art."

Erik's father was a painter, and the interests of the son soon rubbed off on the father. "My dad got into painting geometric shapes and became more curious about science. Science seemed to me something to aspire to because it was more solid than the shifting subjective land of the arts.

"My father thought that I should go to MIT, and I believed him. I wanted to excel and prove myself. There are other places where I probably would have been happier—where I undoubtedly would have been—but there just wasn't a whole lot of decisionmaking going on."

Erik entered MIT in 1974. "At the time, it definitely felt like the sixties were over. In retrospect, though, the whole ethic was still there, in the music and the media: tolerance, free everything, and the idea of creativity and independence being the most important things. But it was everywhere by then, not just on campuses. We were sort of in the suburban equivalent of the sixties," he said.

Erik quickly grew disillusioned. "The male-to-female ratio at MIT was seven to one. The social life was not terrific. The people on my floor were great people, but most of us were disappointed and generally confused about everything."

Lack of female companionship or companionship in general was not the only problem. "As school wore on, I began to realize that there was a conflict in me. I wanted to succeed in this particular area—math and science—which I was good at and enjoyed. But there was also this feeling of still being trapped into performing for my parents, performing for the system, performing for someone else. Part of me wanted to explore, go out and just cut loose from everything, which I had never really done."

After his sophomore year, Erik did just that, traveling around the country in a VW bus. "That was fun, but when I came back to MIT, everything came crashing down. I didn't know if I wanted to be there, I didn't know why I was there, all of the momentum from high school, of succeeding and getting excited about the work, had fizzled out.

"The urge to just leave was there from the beginning. I think the trigger actually came from arguing about it with my parents. They kept asking me what I was going to do if I left college, saying that I was not going to be able to get a job and that my mind would want something to do.

"At some point in the conversation I decided, from something that one of them said, that part of the reason they wanted me there was for them, for their bragging rights, for their feeling of success through me. So I decided to leave after the fall of my junior year, to just go off and do something else."

Once he made the choice to leave, Erik let the decision simmer. "I wasn't really talking to anyone else. In my family, it was important to work things out for yourself. It's also true that at MIT at the time you were given no guidance. You had to succeed on your own. It was very much a part of the place. There was no one to ask for help."

Erik persuaded his parents to give him the money they would have given him for living expenses at school, but that was as far as his planning went. "I basically decided I wasn't going to be in school, and while I fantasized vaguely about doing something else, I didn't really plan for it at all."

Erik said that staying in Cambridge was probably his biggest mistake. "I really cared about my roommate, and we had this apartment that I loved. This was a place that fit me perfectly, and I was afraid that if I left I wouldn't get the room back when I returned. In retrospect, that was really horrible. This was a time when I was taking off to do something for myself, and here I was trapped by this dependence. But I guess that sort of captures the whole situation."

By the time classes started in January, Erik began halfheartedly contemplating what might occupy his time for the next six months.

"I was thinking about getting a job, but again there was no guidance. The academic world was always something separate from the real world, and growing up, I hadn't had any particular model for how you go about getting a job in the real world. I checked the want ads, went to the resource center, and I found virtually nothing. Having gone through this experience quite a few times, I now know that if I had done the right things I could have found a job."

Still, he did not seek help. "I was doing my best to sever ties with my parents, with the institution, with everything I thought was a symbol of authority, so I had my little retreat, my apartment, where I could go and pretty much do what I wanted."

So that's what he did. "I worked on an animated film, I played sitar, took long walks, and just thought, and thought, and thought, and tried to figure out what I was going to do next," he said.

"My feelings about school didn't really change a whole lot, and so part of the whole experience was coming to grips with the fact that what I had done—leaving school—didn't really change anything, and if I was going to take this course, I was really going to have to get a job.

"And then reality started to set in. It wasn't so much a change in direction. I just began to see that going to school was not some grand mission which was going to achieve these lofty goals that I had started with. It was a way to get a job, something I had to do to survive."

That summer, Erik reentered MIT. "Things didn't change much. I guess resigned is the right word for the way I approached it. I basically just got through the last year and a half. Then I got my degree and went to the West Coast to seek what I thought I was going to find in the first place. In those last fifteen months, I felt I was basically just plowing through."

Erik says that he would do many things differently if he had that year to live over again, but he resists calling it a total failure. "I wasn't trying to achieve anything, so in that sense I didn't really fail. The pressure built to a certain point, and I had to stop going to school for a while. But what I needed was a break from what I was doing, so staying in the same situation was self-defeating."

ALEXIS LEVY

Atlanta, Georgia

UNIVERSITY OF GEORGIA '96

While she was growing up, Alexis Levy always enjoyed being one step ahead of the cutting edge, which left her about a hundred steps ahead of most Atlanta teenagers.

"When I was in seventh grade, I bleached my hair white, then dyed it black and it turned this shade of olive green. So all I wore was green to accentuate my hair. In eighth grade, I would wear red on Mondays—red makeup, red clothes, red everything. On Tuesdays, it was yellow—yellow eyeliner, yellow lipstick—just to see what people would do, just to hear them talk about me in the hallways," she recalled.

In high school, it finally occurred to Alexis that most other people her age were more interested in looking like everyone else. "In tenth grade, they turned our school into a middle school and sent us all to our rival high school. At our new school, there were a lot of kids who drove Alfa-Romeos. Being around all those snotty people, some of my friends fell into it. A lot of people chose between whether they would be real or whether they would be accepted, and at age sixteen or seventeen, that's a big deal. I did not like it. I was not a crowd follower at all."

Most students from Alexis's high school went straight to the University of Georgia after they graduated. "I was not going to go to UGA. I told my dad that I was going to go to school out of state, and he said, 'Well, I can't afford it,' and I told him, 'Well, I'll make sure you can afford it.' "

During her junior year of high school, however, Alexis met a boy who convinced her to change her plans altogether. "My friends and I used to hang out at this warehouse where we would go to see our friends play in bands. One night I met this guy named Rick, and I liked him, and we started dating. He was a year older than me, and he had dropped out of high school. He was basically just a fuckup, but that was part of the attraction. He was a rebel, and my parents hated him.

"About midway through my senior year in high school, he decided that he was going to join the army, and I freaked. What was going to happen to me? What about us? So he asked me to marry him."

At that point, warning bells should have gone off in Alexis's head. The summer before her senior year, her family had called a conference one Sunday morning. "I thought they had spent all my college money or something," Alexis recalled.

But, instead, her parents, her grandmother, her thirty-seven-year-old sister, and her thirty-two-year-old brother told her that they had something far more weighty to disclose.

"All my life, they had always made jokes about me being adopted, because I have blue eyes even though no one else in the family does and because I don't like chocolate ice cream. Then they told me that I really was adopted, and that I had been lucky enough to know my mother all my life. She was sitting there at the table.

"I remember asking them what they were talking about. I looked around. It obviously wasn't my mother: It couldn't have been my grandmother. And then I looked at my sister, and I said, 'Don't even tell me it's her,' and they said 'Yes.' "

Alexis's "sister" had married her boyfriend when she was nineteen and given birth to Alexis at age twenty. "They got divorced when I was a baby, and my sister just couldn't take care of me any longer, so they drew up the papers and my parents adopted me. Until I was seventeen years old, I thought I had a mother, father, sister, brother, when I really had a grandma, grandpa, mother, and uncle," she said.

"I cried for a little while. I was kind of frantic. But once I thought about it, I knew that it was much better that my grandparents had raised me themselves, because I wouldn't have had braces, I wouldn't have had dance lessons; I wouldn't be the person I am today. So I'm grateful for that."

So when Alexis faced a marriage proposal at a similarly young age, she had some family history on which to reflect. But, as she recalled, it became remarkably easy to follow in her sister's footsteps.

"I guess I had been with Rick for so long that I just didn't think there was much else out there. He told me that he might be going to Germany or Korea. I figured it would be a good way to get out of Atlanta. The government would pay for our apartment. I wouldn't have to work if I didn't want to. I could live the life, see the sights, and go to school later."

Alexis was determined that she would not end up in the same situation her sister had been in, and her parents decided not to challenge her. "There was no way I was going to get pregnant. I just wouldn't go that route," she said.

"My parents had fought my sister on it, but she rebelled and got married anyway, and they eventually lost contact with her for a long time. They didn't want to push me away, so they told me that they didn't approve but that they knew I was going to do what I wanted to do.

"Looking back on it now, I think part of the attraction was shock value. Everyone would say, 'Did you hear what Alexis is doing? She's getting married. Oh my God!' "

Before anyone had a chance to react much at all, the newlyweds made a quick getaway. "I doubled up on my classes to graduate in March so we could move up to Virginia, where Rick was going to be stationed. I think I actually had to come back for my wedding shower. We got married in a judge's chambers in Alexandria, just the two of us."

Almost immediately after the ceremony, Alexis felt ill at ease. "We got in a fight in the car on the way back from the courthouse. I knew from the first minute that it was not right, but I didn't want to go home with my tail between my legs either. When I called and told my mom, she told me I had made my bed and now I had to lie in it.

"So I was going to be a tough girl and stick it out, but looking at him, I knew I wasn't going to spend the rest of my life with this guy. I just thought it was a more exciting adventure than going off to college like everybody else."

Alexis knew that getting married wasn't the only way to seek adventure at age eighteen, but she wasn't optimistic about her options. "I didn't want to take some tour across Europe with other people my age. I had thought about being an exchange student, but I knew it wasn't going to work out financially."

So Alexis slept in that bed, which her parents had purchased for her and her husband, and tried to make the best of it. "We got an apartment, and I was excited that there were hardwood floors and all, but we didn't realize that it was in a bad neighborhood.

"It was a real eye-opener. The woman who lived upstairs

from us told me that she had killed someone and that she had buried her victim in the woods somewhere. She and her husband both worked at McDonald's, and they had three kids under the age of three. And there I was thinking, this is no life for me."

Alexis soon tired of being a housewife. "I was hanging out at home, watching television. I had to get out of the house. I was picking at things, cleaning them all the time. I was becoming very anal, so I decided to go to the mall and look for a job."

Life with Rick was also a disappointment. "There just wasn't any substance to the boy. He was happy playing Nintendo all day long. I had only spent time with him on the weekends in high school. There were times then when it had been dull, but we would go out to clubs and movies. And, hey, I was with my boyfriend, right?"

Alexis found a job at a clothing store and began working full-time right away. "I found myself overworking just to be away from him, setting opposite hours from him. That was freedom. After a week, they promoted me to assistant manager. I had always been an average student, so that was my first taste of 'Wow, I can do anything I want to.' "

But what she really wanted to do was bail out, and after six months her parents agreed to let her return home. "He begged me to stay, but I told him there was nothing he could do. My brother came up, we rented a U-Haul, and I came home to Atlanta.

"It was a relief to be back. When I saw my parents, I was crying. The whole horribleness was over, and I knew it had been a mistake, and I thanked them for letting me come back and not telling me I told you so and not treating me like a failure. They were very good about it.

"My friend Maria was still in town, and I called her that

first night we got back. That was the night that the Gulf War started, and we went out for doughnuts. I felt like a kid again, eating Dunkin' Donuts at midnight. It felt good."

In the next few months, Alexis finalized her divorce and started dating again. "I got involved with a guy who was into communes and meditation. He was so anti-Establishment, and I was so material—I like my clothes, and I like to go shopping. So there was a lot of discussion and intellectual interaction, which was something I hadn't experienced before. It wasn't 'Let's go play video games.' It was 'Let's think about this issue,' and that made me a bigger person.

"I decided that I was ready to start school again. I had seen what life was like without it. I still didn't want to go to UGA. I did not want to go to college with the same people I went to high school with. College was going to be my clean slate. So I enrolled in DeKalb Community College, which was near my house."

Over the next year, Alexis changed her mind about wanting to graduate in two years with an associate's degree in dental hygiene and decided her real desire was to get a Ph.D. and become a professor. Aside from two B's, she maintained a perfect academic record.

"I was inducted into the national honors society for two-year colleges, and I was the president of our honors program during my second year at DeKalb. It was a big deal to me. I went from being an okay student in high school to being a married teenager to being a representative from my school at a national honors convention."

By then, most of the acquaintances from Alexis's past life had finished school at UGA. When she found a program in health promotion and behavior at the school, she decided to transfer to UGA after she completed her two years at DeKalb.

Her first year in Athens, Alexis maintained a 4.0 grade point average. And she remains convinced that the time off changed her life for the better.

"When you start school as a first-grader, you go through so many changes. It never stops, and there's always the constant involvement in school. You don't get time to think about who you really are," she said.

"You're trying so hard to keep cool, to be cool, to be accepted by your friends, and to stay one step above average in terms of your outward appearance. Then you get out there and interact with people, and you have to learn to be yourself. You can't make excuses. And you learn some hard lessons."

ELIZABETH HUNTER

Ravena, New York

WELLESLEY COLLEGE '92

Elizabeth Hunter has a button on her lapel that says, "Experience is what you get when you didn't get what you wanted."

So what did Elizabeth want? "To get the hell out of Ravena, New York. When I was fourteen years old, I read somewhere that every teenager thinks not only that they live in the most boring place in the universe but that they were handpicked to live there."

Ravena is a small town near Albany, and according to Elizabeth, it was occupied by people with very small minds. "My dad is a United Church of Christ minister, and when you're a PK, a preacher's kid, there's a certain untouchable quality to you.

"Everyone knows who you are. The local drug dealer wouldn't have sold me drugs even if I had wanted them. He was convinced that if you sold drugs to the minister's kid you were damned to hell. There are a lot of people who apologize for swearing in front of you. Crazy shit like that.

"Basically, there are two patterns. Either we become preachers ourselves or we end up in jail."

Elizabeth managed to avoid both fates, however, and ended up in Mexico for her junior year of high school. She returned to Ravena from her foreign study and discovered that little had changed.

"I thought, 'Wow, I'm going home, and things will be comfortable, and they won't be strange or weird.' Then you get home and everything is all strange and weird.

"I was the valedictorian, and this guy who was third in the class, his mom was writing nasty letters to the school paper about me, saying I was given credit for classes that I hadn't taken. It just goes to show what a small town it was that they actually printed them."

At that point, Elizabeth was ready to escape, and she decided to go to Columbia University in New York City. "I considered Boston, but I figured that would be too safe. I had thoughts about being a lawyer. Columbia had a great political science program and the courses in the core curriculum were all classes I wanted to take."

After a year of grinding through the core, she found herself increasingly irritated with life in the classroom.

"There was this paper I was supposed to write about Karl Marx based on three 500-page tomes, none of which I had touched. I read through the index, underlined key words from the essay question, wrote a ten-page paper stringing together all these quotes, and I got an A. The professor said it was the best paper she had seen all term.

"I remember thinking at the time that if I was going to go through this whole college thing just learning how to bullshit my way through papers, well, it seemed to me that I already knew how to do that. I figured they had nothing to teach me. I wasn't really in school; I was just showing up for classes."

After sitting through one particularly uninspired philosophy class, Elizabeth knew she'd had enough. "I walked out and said to the woman walking next to me, 'I just can't sit through another class like that. I'm leaving.'

"I told my mom, and she started to cry. It obviously meant that she was a bad mother. My father has always been the kind of person who will say, 'I think what you're doing is stupid, but when it blows up in your face, I want you to know that you can come to me and let me help you.'

"He said that he hoped I was making the right decision. I told him that I didn't think it really mattered, that this was the only decision I was going to be able to make right now. My mind was made up. It was more important to me that I was committed to living with the decision I had made than wondering if it had been the right one."

When the spring semester ended a few weeks later, Elizabeth packed her bags and moved to Boston. She lived in Fenway House, an MIT-affiliated, independently owned cooperative. The place had a long history of housing assorted offbeat characters from the MIT community.

"Faggots, addicts, and religious fanatics," she said, reciting the unofficial Fenway roster. "The house definitely had its own lore—bizarre sexual practices, long-haired hippie freaks. There used to be a bunch of anarchists who lived there and built bombs, and a radical Communist press in the basement."

Admittedly, it takes a certain spirit to adapt to such surroundings, but at the time, Elizabeth said, it suited her well. "It was one of those groups of people that you run into very few times in your life. You know that you can be absolutely nuts, and the worst thing that will happen to you is that someone will look at you and go, 'You're crazy!' "

By then, Elizabeth's parents had accepted the fact that she wasn't going back to school and had agreed to pay for her housing for the summer. She worked a couple of temporary jobs to earn money, and spent her evenings directing a production of *A Little Night Music*.

"It was wonderful. I was free. No one was expecting me to do anything, and that made all the difference."

As the fall approached, however, Elizabeth had not figured out what she wanted to do next. She had also lost both her jobs.

"I had two jobs. I worked as a receptionist at a software company for about a week. My life got too interesting, so I left that one. Work is that feeling that I have to go somewhere to do something for someone else. Then I worked in a lab for about six weeks and got fired, which was incredibly traumatic.

"I had planned on spending a year in Boston. My friend found us a house at the end of the summer. We decided to call the place 'the restaurant' because it seemed to capture the qualities of both Arlo Guthrie's "Alice's Restaurant" and Douglas Adams's *The Restaurant at the End of the Universe*."

Elizabeth now thinks the place was misnamed. "I lost thirty-seven pounds in the next few months, because I was too poor to afford anything but macaroni and tuna fish," she said.

She earned a meager hourly wage at a local art-supply store. "I did manage to last there. I've been working since I was fourteen years old, and I am capable of holding down a job when it becomes important. I do have the work-eat connection firmly established."

Elizabeth soon began to wonder if staying out of school for an entire year was a good idea. "This is going to sound so shallow, but it basically hit me when I realized that my dad wasn't going to pay my credit-card bills. There was no reason he should have been supporting me—I wasn't holding up my end of the bargain by going to school."

But, she admitted, she never stopped to consider that fact

seriously before she decided to take the year off. "It really hits home when you realize that you make $6.25 an hour before taxes and you have to pay $300 a month in rent. At that point, you really don't have any money. It's hard to do all the simple things that you take for granted."

Elizabeth eventually decided to return to school in January, but she tried hard to erase the notion of having failed from her mind. "It was just reality, not a huge disappointment. There's nothing wrong with self-pity; give yourself a day or two and then do something about it," she said.

Elizabeth thought a change of scene would do her good, so she applied and was accepted at Wellesley College. "I started school and immediately met a professor who became one of the personal gods of my life. She taught a class on ethnicity in American politics, and her thesis was that you can't see the whole picture in any political situation unless you examine how ethnicity plays a role.

"That sounds like a simple thing, but she just added whole new dimensions to the way I thought about things. A part of my mind had been asleep for six months. For seventeen years, I went into a classroom and people said interesting things and asked me to think about them. Then, all of a sudden, I didn't do that for six months, and I missed it so much.

"I think it took going back to realize how bored and restless I had been. I felt that what I had done during my time off was great, but it was time out. I wasn't getting anywhere, which in some ways was really good. I've spent a lot of the rest of my life going somewhere and trying to do things that will make me attractive for this summer job or for this company. Time out allowed me to break that cycle, but it didn't make it any less true that you have to keep moving in your life."

Still, she has few regrets about the meandering path her education took. "I was very self-aware. I knew I would never be eighteen again and would never be able to look at things with those eyes, and so I wanted to look as much as I possibly could. I've always believed that there are no excuses—there are only reasons. And the number-one reason for everything is that it seemed like a good idea at the time."

CHAD HAMMETT

Henderson, Texas

UNIVERSITY OF TEXAS '96

Chad Hammett grew up in Henderson, Texas, a small oil town in the eastern part of the state that boomed and has since gone bust. When his parents got divorced while he was in high school, Chad started working a string of odd jobs to earn his own spending money.

Because his mother had also started working more to make up for his father's absence, Chad felt that getting a job was the least he could do to pitch in. "My mom was an elementary-school teacher, and she had to take a night job at a bakery to make ends meet," he said.

Chad delivered pizzas until his car broke down, picked up golf balls at a golf driving range, and worked in the bookstore of a nearby community college.

Seeing his mother's financial struggles helped convince Chad he wanted to get the best college education possible. "Here's a woman who has a college education," he said, "and just to be able to support her children, she needs to work a kind of manual-labor job that doesn't take very many skills."

Chad graduated from high school in 1990 and went directly on to the University of Texas at Austin. He was overwhelmed at first by the sheer size of the school and its student body. "UT is the second-largest university in the country, with over 50,000 undergraduate and graduate students. It's easy to feel lost," he said.

Nevertheless, Chad seemed to adjust well. He had been a standout member of his debate team in high school, and joining UT's speech team was a perfect extracurricular activity for him. A new girlfriend also eased the adjustment to college life. "I had a real straitlaced girlfriend, and she was into hanging out together to watch movies and study a lot. I made all A's and B's that semester."

Their relationship also indirectly led to Chad's desire to become a writer. "The real impetus for my writing came at the end of the first semester of my freshman year. I was horribly dumped by this girl and really didn't have anybody to talk to. I just turned to my notebook and wrote and wrote."

Chad said he was doing okay at UT until halfway through the first semester of his sophomore year. "Trouble began when I started getting all these pre-approved credit-card applications. Visa, MasterCard, Discover, they all sent me offers."

The credit cards enabled Chad to pay for his expenses when he traveled with the speech team. He also used the cards to get cash advances to pay the rent on his off-campus apartment.

"I also started partying a lot," Chad said. "My friends and I would go out and meet girls and drink almost every night. Usually we drank whatever was cheapest, bottom-of-the-barrel wine or a plastic bottle of vodka mixed with Kool-Aid."

Chad was becoming increasingly depressed. "I started

drinking when nobody else was there," he recalled. "Sometimes I didn't feel like going out at all. I would just sit around and watch TV.

"If I stayed up late partying on a Sunday night, my intention each time was 'Okay, I'm going to get up for class Monday morning. I'm going to set the alarm and go.' Then I'd hit that snooze button, turn off the alarm, and never make it to class."

Chad hit the snooze button one time too many during the spring of his sophomore year. When he woke up, he had a GPA of 0.0 for the semester. "I still don't even really know what happened," he said.

Chad always planned to regain control of things. "I thought, 'No problem, I'll go to class on Tuesday. I'll get the notes from somebody. The professor will let me retake that quiz. On Thursday, I'll talk to that professor and say, "I'm sorry I missed that assignment. Is there any way I can make it up?" '

"Tuesday rolled into Thursday, and before I knew it, I had slept through my Monday-morning class again. Next thing I knew, it was mid-April, and I hadn't been to class for over a month. I didn't go back the rest of the semester."

Chad didn't even open the envelope from the registrar's office when his grades for the semester arrived. "I didn't want to look inside," he said.

His plan for the summer was to move into a new apartment with a friend and find a job that would allow him to pay off his credit-card debt. Finding employment was difficult in a town with tens of thousands of students and a limited number of cash registers and coffee shops. Meanwhile, the check for his security deposit bounced, his credit cards were near their limit, and the rent was due.

"I hocked pretty much all my stuff, my CD player, everything," he said. "I even went home and got my baseball cards. I sold all my Nolan Ryan and George Brett cards, because I knew that would be a quick way to make money.

"I remember thinking to myself, 'Hey, there's no good reason for me to be in school right now.' " So he packed up and moved home to Houston, where his mother was living.

The original plan was to take one semester off from school. "I figured I would have a better chance of finding a job at home. I could work for a couple of months, make a couple of payments on my credit card, pay my friend what I still owed for the apartment, and be ready to go back to school. But it's not that easy to catch up."

Chad spent the next three semesters living at home and working at Macys, a department store in a nearby mall. "Here I am, I can read and write and should be in school, but I'm not. Being around my friends who were still in school during their vacations was especially hard. I thought I was a failure," he said.

While living at home, Chad started to become closer to his family. "Before, I saw my family only in terms of how they affected me, not as actual people with lives of their own. Spending more time with them when I was older helped me begin to look at them in a different way."

Chad was especially grateful to his mother for her help in overcoming the hardest part of working at Macys: the need for dependable transportation. "There were days when they would call up and say, 'We need you to come in.' I would have to say, 'Well, I can't, because the bus doesn't run this late or that early.' My mom always gave me rides and sometimes lent me her car. I wouldn't have been able to do it without her."

Chad decided to go back to the University of Texas in the

spring of 1994. By then, he had paid off most of his $3,000 credit-card debt and been awarded financial aid.

"I started looking around me at the mall. I saw a lot of unhappy people in their thirties working there. They would say, 'I'm going back to school one of these days. I'm taking one class a year at the community college.' There's nothing wrong with that; it's just not what I wanted for myself."

Returning to school was easy. "Being twenty-three or twenty-four when the people in your classes are nineteen and twenty is no big deal," Chad said. "It makes you more of a sage than a loser."

He plans to graduate in May of 1996 and is thinking of applying to graduate-school programs in creative writing. Being back in school is a whole different ball game for him now. "I was walking through the stacks in the library, and I asked myself, 'As a hopeful writer, is there a better place to be? I've got two rows of American literature by authors starting with the letter C right here.' "

Chad has transferred what he learned working at Macys to what he calls his "job" as a student. "I never miss work and I'm never late. I know that if I don't show up and I don't call and accept responsibility, they're going to catch me on it and I'm going to be fired.

"What I've had to do is force myself to act as though the same rules apply for school. School is like work, and being a student is my job," he said.

Chad is combining his studies with a part-time job at a clothing store in Austin. His experience at Macys helped him beat out dozens of other students who were applying for the same position. "They started me off at $8 an hour, and my salary increases each time I sell over 15 percent of my sales target," he said. "Were it not for stepping out for two years, I would never have had this kind of job and been able to pay for school.

"If you think it's your right to be in college, you'll find out real quickly that it's not. But if you think of it as a privilege you have earned through your own hard work, you'll enjoy it a lot more."

APPENDIX

RESOURCES

General Resources 262

Work

Finding a job or
internship abroad 264
Teaching English abroad 265
Working abroad as an au
pair 267
Working on a cruise
ship or yacht 268
Community service
abroad 269
Internships and jobs in
the U.S. 271
Community Service in
the U.S. 273
Jobs in the outdoors 274
Environmental activism 276

Working on a kibbutz in
Israel 277
Working on a scientific
or archaeological
expedition 278

Travel

Travel Abroad 279
Travel in the U.S. 281
Traveling on a bicycle 281

Study

Post-graduate academic
years in the U.S. 283
Academic programs
abroad/learning a foreign
language abroad 283

To help you begin to plan your time off, we have included this directory of publications, programs, and organizations you might find useful. The best place to begin is always a college or university career center, or the local library, where there is lots of information and all of it is free. Try to visit at least two or three bookstores, too. Check the sections on college guides, careers, travel, and anything else that seems at all relevant. If something in our directory interests you and you can't find it in a bookstore or library, call the publisher or source that offers it. Publishers' telephone numbers are listed in a reference book called *Books in Print*, which is available at most libraries and bookstores. Many of the publishers and organizations listed here will let you order books directly over the phone.

Your public, college, or high school librarians should be able to get books for you through interlibrary loan if they don't have it in their collection. Finally, if you think you've found a program or position that fits your needs, call and ask for the names of some people who have done it before. Often, the best way to find out about a certain experience is to talk to someone who has had it himself. And remember, our directory is only the tip of the iceberg. There is a world of possibilities out there which you can investigate on your own.

One of the best ways to access this world these days is through the World Wide Web on the Internet. Our website, www.takingtimeoff.com, has dozens of links to people and places that can help you plan your time off.

GENERAL RESOURCES

Publications

Time Out: Taking a Break from School to Travel, Work, and Study in the U.S. and Abroad, by Robert Gilpin and Caroline Fitzgibbons. Simon & Schuster, 1992. This book is chock-full of options for an academic year in the U.S. or abroad, post-graduate programs at secondary schools, work opportunities in the U.S. and abroad, internships, travel/study programs, language study and cultural exchange programs, and community service programs.

Work, Study, Travel Abroad: The Whole World Handbook, by the Council on International Educational Exchange Staff (CIEE). St. Martin's Press, 1994. Includes a strong region-by-region guide to creating opportunities for yourself all over the world.

Alternatives to the Peace Corps: A Directory of Third World and U.S. Volunteer Opportunities, edited by Annette Olson. Institute for Food & Development Policy, Food First Books, 1994. Includes helpful sections on evaluating organizations and bringing the lessons that you have learned back home. Also contains an excellent resource section.

Jobs in Paradise, by Jeffrey Maltzman. HarperCollins Publishers, 1993. Lists more than 200,000 jobs in the U.S., Canada, South Pacific, and Caribbean, including jobs associated with adventure travel, skiing, mountaineering, beaches, deserts, rivers, lakes, amusement parks, and cruise ships.

What Color Is Your Parachute? A Practical Manual for Job Hunters and Career Changers, by Richard Nelson Bolles. Ten Speed Press, 1995. While most people describe this as a career book, it's a good read for anyone who is feeling generally confused about what the next twelve months—or twelve years—may hold.

International Directory of Voluntary Work, by Roger Brown and David Woodworth. Peterson's Guides, 1993. Describes hundreds of agencies offering jobs, as well as qualifications and conditions. Particularly strong on Britain and Europe.

Programs & Organizations

Center for Interim Programs. This organization, run by highly regarded educator Cornelius Bull, has been helping students for over fifteen years to create a time-off plan to match their needs. A former teacher and headmaster, Bull has compiled a vast database of internship, travel, study, and volunteer possibilities. After a free initial consultation, students pay a fee and work with Bull to plan their time off. He is known for the individual attention he gives to students. (617) 547-0980

CIEE (Council on International Educational Exchange). An incredibly helpful organization that has many publications for people who want to work, travel, or study abroad. Call for a current catalogue of publications. (212) 661-1414

Council Travel. This travel agency, with offices in most large cities and college towns, specializes in students traveling on the cheap. They know more about getting to faraway places cheaply than just about anyone.

International Youth Hostel Federation. IYHF runs a worldwide network of hostels where you can stay inexpensively and meet other travelers. (202) 783-6161

Transitions Abroad. An excellent resource for students who wish to spend time abroad in any capacity. Its *Alternative Travel Directory* is a well-organized guide to working, traveling, studying, and living abroad. The organization also publishes a bimonthly magazine called *Transitions Abroad: The Guide to Learning, Living and Working Overseas*. It also has many other resources available. 1-800-293-0373

The Venture Consortium. A collection of colleges and universities that maintain well-stocked resource centers for students who want to take time off. The following schools are in the consortium: Bates College, Brown University, College of the Holy Cross, Swarthmore College, Vassar College, and Wesleyan University. It may be difficult to get assistance from Venture if you do not attend these schools; try to talk your own school into becoming affiliated with the Consortium. The central office is at Brown. (401) 863-2324

WORK

FINDING A JOB OR INTERNSHIP ABROAD

Looking for international work can seem a daunting task. However, there are plenty of interesting work experiences available around the world, and you already have the only two qualifications that are required: a desire to work and a knowledge of the English language. You shouldn't feel constrained if you don't arrange your job or internship before you leave. Many interesting jobs (with pay!) surface only after you arrive at your destination. Australian travelers are famous for their ability to wander the globe for years, stringing together jobs along their journeys.

This section gives a thorough listing of the best resource guides for finding work abroad. Before you go, you may also want to talk with people who have been to your destination. Once you are in the country, your guidebooks, particularly the Lonely Planet series, can be very useful in telling you where to find the local "Help Wanted" ads. Check the local English-language papers as well for job possibilities. Other travelers and expatriates can be a great source of information and contacts on where to go and who to talk to. Before leaving, you should also contact the foreign embassy in Washington, D.C., and through them the tourism bureau of the countries you are interested in.

Many countries require prospective employees to obtain a work permit and an immigration visa showing that employment has been approved by local government authorities. It will usually not be possible to change from a tourist visa to a work visa while in a foreign country. If you can arrange your job and the necessary paperwork ahead of time, by all means do so. Council Travel and other specialized student travel agencies will be able to provide you with the latest information on work regulations around the world.

Keep in mind that in some countries the employment process is very informal, and you won't need a work permit or other bureaucratic paperwork. Some travelers take jobs as waiters or temps and are paid in cash under the table.

If you have a specific job in mind, do your research before you venture off into the wild blue yonder. Write letters to organizations that suit your interests, and be persistent. Give specific dates when you will be available to work and offer as much supporting information about yourself as possible. Because you will not have an opportunity to meet prospective employers in person before they hire you, draw a very clear picture of who you are and why you want to work for them. If you are willing to work for free, emphasize this in your first contact with the organization. The unpaid internship is a phenomenon that has not hit other countries the way it has the United

States. Many organizations you contact will be thrilled at their good fortune to have an enthusiastic, unpaid worker in their midst.

Publications

Work Your Way Around the World, by Susan Griffith. Peterson's Guides, 1995. Includes country-by-country descriptions of how to find short-term job opportunities abroad. A fantastic book.

Working Abroad. Information on paying jobs and au pair placement in Europe. Available free from InterExchange, an organization in New York City that will arrange work permits, housing, and job placements for a fee. (212) 924-0446

Passport to Overseas Employment, by Dale Chambers. Prentice Hall, 1990. Includes country-by-country work-permit requirements, employment opportunities with the UN, the U.S. government, airlines, cruise lines, and tourist organizations.

Vacation Work publishes a *Live and Work in* . . . series which includes many European countries and covers employment, housing, and starting a business. It also offers a book called *Working in Ski Resorts—Europe.* These books are distributed in America by Peterson's Guides.

Opportunities in Africa, by the African-American Institute. This resource book provides a comprehensive list of organizations with paid and unpaid work opportunities in Africa. Distributed by Interbook. (212) 566-1944

Programs & Organizations

People to People International. Arranges unpaid internships in London, Dublin, Moscow, Paris, Prague, and other foreign cities. (816) 531-4701

TEACHING ENGLISH ABROAD

Teaching English is one of the most accessible and popular options for working abroad. Although you might not have any teaching or tutoring experience, your eighteen-plus years of speaking English is your most sought-after "credential." And private individuals, schools, hotels, and universities all over the globe would love to have you teach.

Why do people in countries from Albania to Zambia want to learn English? Basically, because English is the lingua franca of international business, tourism, diplomacy, and higher education. And you are benefiting from the classic supply-and-demand model: there are loads of people who want to learn English, and, in most places, there are very few native speakers who can teach it.

If you are nervous about leaving the country without having arranged a position, there are many programs that will hire you here in the United States for teaching positions abroad. Your potential employer might even pay for your air ticket in advance. If you feel more adventurous, you can wing it. Generally, you should have no problem securing an English-teaching position in most countries after your arrival. Teaching and tutoring positions are often advertised in local English-language newspapers. You can also visit language academies and, if you are very ambitious, advertise in the local papers and at the universities. Although teaching salaries will vary, you will generally make enough money to support yourself in the country. Some places will pay quite well, but these areas may have high living expenses. If your main motivation is to make lots of cash, you will probably be disappointed. However, even if you have to tap into your savings account, you'll still be spending far less than you would if you were studying or traveling abroad.

You may be required to teach for a minimum of one year in certain programs, so investigate all your options before making any commitments. Particularly if you had your ticket paid for by the organization, it might not let you out of your contract without some penalty. It's generally not a good idea to accept a position knowing that you are going to bail out after the first week.

Working conditions may be less than perfect for a novice English teacher like yourself. Teaching resources may be limited, so be prepared to be creative in your instruction methods in the more off-the-beaten-track locales. Playing charades can only take you so far, however. When you see all those bright, eager "teach me" faces in your classroom, you may wish you had a little more training. If you know that you will be in a situation like this, and you feel inspired, you may want to pack an English grammar book and a work-book. And don't forget your English–(Insert your country's language here) dictionary.

By spending a significant period of time living and working in a foreign country, you can get a great sense of the country's culture. This is particularly true if you have some knowledge of the host country's language and you are living among the local people. Some schools may even arrange for your housing with a family or in a guesthouse. One last thing—don't be nervous if you failed your high school foreign-language class. Proficiency in the local language is rarely a requirement for obtaining a position. As a general rule, however, your overall experience in a country will be more enjoyable if you learn your host country's language.

Publications

Teaching English Abroad: Talk Your Way Around the World!, by Susan Griffith. Peterson's Guides, 1994. Includes a 250-page country-by-country guide to finding jobs, and a helpful guide to training and preparing for your job.

Teaching English Abroad. This book is a bible for people interested in teaching English abroad. Published by Transitions Abroad, it contains listings of specific programs around the world. 1-800-293-0373

Now Hiring! Jobs in Asia: The Insider's Guide to Gaining Seasonal & Year-Round Employment Throughout Asia, by Steve Gutman, Clarke Can-field, and Debra Steinberg. Perpetual Press, 1993. This book focuses mostly on English-teaching jobs. Jam-packed with useful information on specific employers.

Teaching English in Asia, by Galen Harris Valle. Pacific View Press, 1995. Includes a helpful section with country-by-country guidelines. Also con-tains useful sections on what makes a good teacher and activities to do with your students.

The Asia Employment Program. Covers only teaching jobs. Published by Progressive Media. 1-800-959-1605

Eastern Europe. A new book on teaching English in Eastern Europe is forth-coming from Progressive Media. 1-800-959-1605

Programs & Organizations

Japan Exchange Teaching Program. The Japanese government sponsors the JET program to encourage cross-cultural exchanges between its citizens and foreigners. JET offers one-year programs for assistant language teachers and coordinators for international relations. Applications are due the December preceding the year you want to go. For more information, call the Japanese Embassy or one of its consulates. (202) 939-6700 for the embassy, or 1-800-463-6538 for an application.

WORKING ABROAD AS AN AU PAIR

For leave-takers on a budget who are dying to get to Europe, working as an au pair is one of the most cost-effective ways to pull it off. Though the job description varies somewhat by country, most au pairs are assigned to a family and work about thirty hours a week taking care of children. In return, they receive their own room and board, weekends and some weekdays off, and a couple of hundred dollars a month in spending money. It's a great way to improve your foreign-language skills and experience real life someplace else. and it's not just for women either. Though most au pairs are women, many men have had successful au pair experiences.

But you should know exactly what you are getting into before you leave. "The most important thing to avoid is getting yourself into a situation where you end up a maid," said Michael Howard, the director of Accord Cultural Exchange. "Many European mothers work forty hours a week and don't have time for housework. While they may say they want an au pair, they may really be looking for a housekeeper." Not surprisingly, Howard says the best way to avoid this situation is to find a family through a reputable agency like his. He promises that his affiliated offices in Europe will find au pairs a new family to work for if they arrive and find that the situation is not work-ing. This happens about twenty percent of the time—a pretty high number.

Howard explains that some of this can be chalked up to spoiled children who are unwilling to be disciplined by their au pair.

Sometimes, though, it's the au pairs who are unprepared. "You have to be aware that there is going to be some culture shock. European families are different from ours, and you have to get used to that," Howard added. "You have to be independent enough to make quick decisions on your own with three kids screaming in the background. It's a lot of responsibility. The question you have to ask yourself is: Are you going for the right reason? If you want to improve your language skills, experience another culture, and you really like children, you'll have an amazing experience. If you're going to Paris because you just fell in love, you'll be doing a disservice to both the family and yourself."

Publications

The Au Pair and Nanny's Guide to Working Abroad, by Susan Griffith and Sharon Legg. Information on how to prepare for and find a child-care job in another country, including a directory of agencies worldwide. Some of this information is included in Griffith's *Work Your Way Around the World*. These books are both under the Vacation Work imprint, available from Peterson's Guides.

Programs & Organizations

Au Pair Abroad: World Learning. Au pair placements for young Americans. (202) 408-5480

Accord Cultural Exchange. Au pair placements in Austria, France, Germany, Italy, and Spain. ACE charges $1,800 for a full-year placement and $750 for a summer job. In addition to placing au pairs with families all over Europe, ACE also offers a "demi-pair" program in Paris. Demi-pairs get room and board and are required to take care of a family's children for fifteen hours a week, about half the usual weekly responsibility. If your French is good enough (four years of high school French or a year or two of college study should suffice), ACE will find you an internship with a multinational company. (415) 386-6203

WORKING ON A CRUISE SHIP OR YACHT

Finding a job on a cruise ship is a science. The standards, first of all, are incredibly high, so this won't be like applying for a summer job running the copy machine or working at the mall. "The cruise industry picks the cream of the crop," Mary Fallon Miller, the author of *How to Get a Job with a Cruise Line,* told us. "They don't want to get out to the middle of the Pacific and discover they picked the wrong people." Still, she explained, that doesn't mean that students with limited work experience should give up without trying.

First, it's important to apply for specific jobs. Lots of clueless people write to cruise lines requesting any available position, and their résumés tend to get cast aside. There are several jobs within your grasp. Most cruises have youth counselors to plan activities for the kids on board. Working in the gift shop, as the "purser's assistant" (like a front-desk job at a hotel), or in the excursion department (coordinating and selling tours at the various ports where the cruise ship stops for an afternoon) are also possibilities. According to Miller, it's tough to get a job as a waiter or busboy on a cruise unless it's an American line, and even those jobs are difficult to come by. Most lines prefer Europeans for those jobs, since training for waiters is more formal there.

"They tend to hire people who make it easy to hire them," Miller explained. "You have to remember that their goal is to make cruises memorable and fun for the passengers. They want to see commitment and follow-through on the idea that the customer comes first, so tailor your past work experience to express that on your résumé. Do your homework on the job you are aiming for. Once you've applied, send a follow-up postcard, since calling the cruise lines can be difficult."

Publications

How to Get a Job with a Cruise Line: Adventure—Travel—Romance: How to Sail Around the World on Luxury Cruise Ships & Get Paid for It, by Mary Fallon Miller. Ticket to Adventure, 1994. Includes tips from cruise-line employees.

The Cruise and Travel Employment Program: The Complete Guide to Finding Employment in the Cruise, Land Tour, and Airline Industries. Progressive Media. 1-800-959-1605

The Hitchhiker's Guide to the Oceans: Crewing Around the World, by Alison Bennet and Claire Davis. Seven Seas Press. A guide to finding jobs on private yachts and cruising vessels around the world.

COMMUNITY SERVICE ABROAD

Unless you have worked and saved up some money, your best bet here will be finding an agency or organization that will give you room and board in exchange for work. One of the best ways to do this is through the Council on International Educational Exchange, which connects people to service projects all over the world for a $195 placement fee. When investigating the possibilities, you should keep a couple of things in mind.

First of all, what do you hope to get out of it? Working on a community-service project is terrific if you want to experience another culture, build your team skills, and make new friends. If you want to learn a real skill, though —say, construction—you may find that difficult. "Our projects aren't designed with an expert on hand to teach you a trade," said Bettina Mok, the program coordinator of CIEE's international volunteer programs.

"You need to be flexible. Go with low or no expectations," Mok added. "Some people expect us to have arranged travel to remote parts of Africa for them, but finding your way there is often just as much of an adventure as participating in the project. Remember also that you'll be working in communities that are really different. In the Netherlands, people don't work any longer than they do here, but they take six really long coffee breaks each day, so the workday actually lasts twelve hours. In Ghana, it might take weeks for the tools or building materials to show up. We hope people are able to take advantage of their location and find other things to do."

Some organizations may require you to pay more than just a placement fee to participate in their programs. This may well run into the thousands of dollars if it's a three- to twelve-month program that includes travel and room and board. "Make sure that it's not a for-profit venture but a service project that actually benefits the community," Mok said, noting that she's heard about a number of for-profit programs like this. The best way to find out is to ask the program for the names of people who have participated in the past.

Publications

Volunteer! The Comprehensive Guide to Voluntary Service in the U.S. and Abroad. Available from the Council on International Educational Exchange.

International Volunteer Projects. Booklet published by the Council on International Educational Exchange.

Beyond Safaris: A Guide to Building People-to-People Ties with Africa, by Kevin Danaher. Covers a wide range of study, environmental, and government programs. Available from Global Exchange. (415) 255-7296

Programs & Organizations

Amigos de las Américas. Interns, age sixteen and up, work for four to eight weeks as summer volunteers on public-health projects in Latin America. 1-800-231-7796

International Christian Youth Exchange—Volunteers Exchange International. ICYE arranges year-long home stays that involve participants in community-service projects around the world. (212) 206-7307

Interns for Peace. A community-sponsored program dedicated to building trust among Jews and Arabs in Israel through a variety of projects. (212) 319-4545

Operation Crossroads Africa. Volunteers work to build community facilities in developing countries. (212) 870-2106

Overseas Development Network. ODN offers internships with community organizations which support local initiatives for economic development. Publications are also available. (415) 431-4204

Partnership for Service Learning. Offers combined study and intercultural experience through community service. Destinations include the Czech Republic, Ecuador, Britain, France, India, Israel, Mexico, and the Philippines. (212) 986-0989

Peace Corps. Volunteers serve for twenty-seven months and receive intensive language training and cultural orientation. Room and board is provided, and a stipend is awarded at the end of service. The Peace Corps has projects throughout the world. 1-800-424-8580

UNIPAL (Universities Educational Fund for Palestinian Refugees). Sends volunteers to teach English to Palestinians and help with handicapped children in the Occupied Territories and Jordan. Unit 410, London House, 19 Old Court Pl., London W8 4PL, England.

Volunteers for Peace. VFP organizes work camps in the U.S. and abroad. Each summer, small groups of young people ₁from around the world come together in European countries and elsewhere to work on community-service projects. VFP work camps involve construction, restoration, agricultural and maintenance projects. After you pay a registration fee and pay for your transportation to the camp, your room, board, and weekend trips are covered. Ask for their publication, *International Workcamp Directory.* (802) 259-2759

World Teach. Helps students obtain volunteer teaching jobs in developing countries. Undergrads who lack a bachelor's degree are eligible for summer-term placements. World Teach also publishes a useful pamphlet, *Fundraising Suggestions for World Teach Volunteers.* (617) 495-5527

INTERNSHIPS AND JOBS IN THE U.S.

There are countless jobs and internships available each year in the United States. If you have never had to look for a job before, don't worry. Though most employers (those at your standard mall job, for instance) say they want to hire people with experience, if you can prove to them that you are a conscientious and á quick learner they'll often be willing to give you a shot. Give them the name of a former teacher or guidance counselor who can serve as a reference (make sure to ask this person first if it's okay to give out his or her name and number), and offer to work on a two-week trial basis. Temping is another option for younger job-seekers. Temporary-employment agencies have all sorts of jobs available—everything from manual labor (helping a business move, for a day or two, for instance) to office work. If you're a good typist or have great phone skills, you can make a lot of money as a temporary secretary or receptionist.

Unpaid internships are a good route to go if you are just looking for experience or have another job that pays your bills. You will find plenty of good internships listed in the annual books put out by Arco, Peterson's Guides, and others. *Princeton Review* also publishes an annual book on the hundred best internships in America. But if there's someplace you want to work and you can't find it listed anywhere, don't worry. Many people we talked to simply called the business or organization where they wanted to work and asked for an unpaid position. Most employers have a hard time turning down someone who is willing to work for free. They'll have an even harder time if you've done your homework and figured out specific tasks that you know they need additional help with. Every business and organization has a backlog of projects that need completing; see if you can find out what they are before you apply. While taking an unpaid internship means that you will have a harder time making ends meet, consider interning for twenty or thirty hours a week and taking a paid job for another thirty to forty hours a week. It's a lot of hours, but this is the best way to get good experience while staving off starvation. Even if your organization of choice brings you in as the king of the photocopying machine, once they see everything else you can do, they may be willing to turn you loose on more interesting projects. If you prove yourself and someone in a paid position leaves while you're there, guess who they'll look to as a replacement? You.

Publications

The National Directory of Internships, by Garrett Martin and Barbara Baker. National Society for Experiential Education, 1993. Includes a great list of other information clearinghouses. (919) 787-3263

How the Military Will Help You Pay for College: The High School Student's Guide to ROTC, the Academies & Special Programs, by Don Betterton. Peterson's Guides, 1990. Discusses both the ROTC/service academy route and entering the armed forces before going to college.

Peterson's *Careers Without College* Series. Peterson's Guides. This series includes information on getting a job in construction, auto mechanics, emergency medicine, fitness, health care, and music. Even if you don't want to make a career of any of these professions, they are all a good way to make money and learn some useful skills during your time off.

The Temp Track: Make One of the Hottest Job Trends of the 90s Work for You, by Peggy O'Connell Justice. Peterson's Guides, 1993. Includes an excellent self-assessment section for people who are unsure whether they are cut out for frequent job changes.

Programs & Organizations

Dynamy. Dynamy is an internship program in Worcester, Massachusetts, for high school graduates. Participants live in Worcester and work in a variety of internships in the community over a nine-month period. (508) 755-2571

Modeling Agencies. Elite is one of the biggest modeling agencies in the United States, with offices in most major cities. It's often easier to break into the business at a smaller agency and work your way up, however. You may also have better luck in New York City, where there are many large agencies.

COMMUNITY SERVICE IN THE U.S.

For those of you who are ready to check out of your house but not ready to check into a college dorm, there are amazing volunteer opportunities both in your hometown and in other parts of the country. Not only will you have the satisfaction of making a social contribution; your experience will also be viewed favorably by future employers and college-admissions officers.

To have the best possible experience, do your research before plunging into a project and committing forty hours a week. Make sure the organization is well run and will use you and your skills effectively. Specifically, look at the time commitment and the type of work you will be doing for the project. Talk to other volunteers in the organization, because this is probably your best route to finding out how your time will be spent. Also, do a realistic self-assessment of your skills and interests and seek out projects that would be a good match. For example, if you are very interested in international issues, you may enjoy the cross-cultural interactions in teaching English to new immigrants. If you are happiest when you are with your golden retriever, you might want to volunteer at your local animal shelter. In general, when you are satisfied with your contribution to the project, you will do better work for the organization and have a more enjoyable experience.

A good place to research your volunteer options is at a local umbrella organization. In some cities, umbrella oranizations such as the United Way will keep a listing of local community-service projects needing additional volunteers. These organizations will match the interests and abilities of would-be volunteers with local needs whenever possible. You should also consult the Yellow Pages to find individual places which accept volunteers. Even organizations that have a professional staff may accept volunteers. Look under "Social Service Organizations," "Handicapped and Disabled Services," "Hospitals," etc. Local religious institutions are also a good resource. We have included some suggestions of programs that you may want to look into.

Publications

Volunteer! The Comprehensive Guide to Voluntary Service in the U.S. and Abroad. Available from the Council on International Educational Exchange. See page 263 for more information on CIEE.

*A **Student's Guide to Volunteering,*** by Theresa Digeronimo. Career Press, 1995. Includes sections on education, the environment, health care, and politics. The book ends with a helpful geographic directory.

Programs & Organizations

American Friends Service Committee. The AFSC is a Quaker organization which has a list of volunteer service possibilities. (215) 241-7295

City Year. City Year is an urban service corps in seven cities around the country. Participants aged seventeen to twenty-three receive a small weekly stipend and a $5,000 educational award at the end of nine months. Corps sites include Boston; Chicago; Columbia, South Carolina; Columbus, Ohio; Providence, Rhode Island; San Antonio; and San Jose. Call the national headquarters for application information. (617) 451-0699

Frontier Nursing Service. FNS couriers live in rural Appalachia and perform home health-care rounds with traveling nurses. Couriers also do chores and assorted grunt work in and around the FNS clinic in Wendover, Kentucky. Room and board are provided. (606) 672-2318

Habitat for Humanity. Habitat builds affordable housing for low-income families. Call 1-800-HABITAT for information on local chapters.

Volunteers in Service to America. VISTA is now part of the federal government's Corporation for National Service. Participants live and work in communities where they help develop grass-roots initiatives to assist the people who live there. Pay is about $650 a month, including health insurance, with a year-end bonus of about $4,700 to put toward higher education. 1-800-424-8867

Youth Service America. A national clearinghouse for information on youth service in the United States. It can put you in touch with service projects in your geographic area. (202) 296-2992

Youth with a Mission. YWAM sends high school and college-aged youth on Christian missions around the world. Programs emphasize hands-on service projects as well as spreading the Gospel. They offer a book called *Stepping Out,* which is all about going on a mission. Ask for their *Go Manual,* which lists missions all over the world. You must attend their Discipleship Training School before going on a mission. (503) 364-3837

JOBS IN THE OUTDOORS

If you prefer to spend your days counting salmon runs in the rivers of the Pacific Northwest, rebuilding trails in the national forests, or educating the public about the wonders of the Grand Canyon as you stand on its rim pointing out various geological features, then working outdoors is for you. Quite often you can even earn a small daily stipend, in addition to housing and food, by working for one of the federal land-management agencies, such as the Forest Service or the National Park Service, or for a university research program or a trail group like the Appalachian Mountain Club.

Working for a federal land-management agency can be exciting and give you an excellent understanding of how federal agencies work. To work for the Forest Service, National Park Service, Bureau of Land Management, or Fish and Wildlife Service, you can apply directly to the volunteer coordinator for a particular national forest, park, or wildlife refuge, or you can go through a feeder service such as the Student Conservation Association. Joining a university's research program for summer fieldwork allows you to gain scientific skills and understanding that will serve you well in academic settings. Simply call large universities in the regions you would like to work in and speak with people in the natural resources, biology, forestry, and agricultural departments. Working for a trail club is an excellent opportunity to get to know a piece of land intimately and assist visitors in experiencing the outdoors. Groups like the Appalachian Mountain Club hire people to spend ten days at a time hiking the famous Appalachian Trail and maintaining their system of huts and shelters.

Publications

The following books are available from Progressive Media. 1-800-959-1605

The Resort Employment Program. Covers theme parks, dude ranches, beach resorts, and other U.S. vacation spots.

The Outdoor Employment Program. Covers U.S. national parks and forests and the private companies that run the hotels and restaurants on park land.

Ski Resorts Job Guide. Covers ski resorts in the U.S.

Programs & Organizations

The Alaska Employment Program. Covers processing and harvesting companies in the fishing industry. Don't be fooled by ads in the back of the college newspapers that say you can make $20,000 in one summer. It happens, but only if you work a hundred hours a week on a boat in dangerous conditions and get very lucky with your catch. More likely, you'll be gutting and canning fish in a factory and make somewhere between $3,000 and $5,000 for a three- to four-month period.

Breckenridge Outdoor Education Center. In return for room and board, volunteers at BOEC teach groups of physically and emotionally disabled people to ski, swim, canoe, and camp. You must be certified in advanced CPR and first aid. (303) 453-6422

California Conservation Corps. The CCC brings California residents between the ages of eighteen and twenty-three together for a year-long program of outdoor service projects. Students receive minimum wage, subsidized housing, and a small stipend. (916) 445-8183

Club Med. Club Med has job opportunities of varying lengths at their luxury resorts around the world. They hire year-round for positions ranging from snorkeling instructors to tour guides. This probably won't be the greatest cultural experience of your life, but it should be a lot of fun. You must be at least nineteen years old and willing to go anywhere in the world to work. The Club Med job hotline is (407) 337-6660

Conservation International. Accepts volunteers to work with local people to conserve rain forests in Botswana, Brazil, Colombia, Costa Rica, Indonesia, and other countries. (202) 429-5660

National Park Service. Seasonal and temporary jobs in national parks across the U.S. (202) 208-4648

The Student Conservation Association. SCA interns work with federal land agencies and private natural-resource organizations. Ask for its publication *Job-Scan.* (603) 543-1700

ENVIRONMENTAL ACTIVISM

Investigating nuclear power plants, rallying against pollution and toxic waste, petitioning federal agencies to change their ways: opportunities to work for the environment are tailor-made for people looking to learn more about how our democratic system works, and gain valuable work experience. The environmental movement runs on the help of thousands of research assistants, policy analysts, interns, and volunteers who sign up for three to twelve months of intensive activity. While stuffing envelopes or canvassing for petition signatures may not seem glamorous, the right type of experience can expose you to a world of opportunities that will help you focus career objectives or land a job someday.

The environmental movement breaks into three different tiers: national, regional, and local non-profits and associations. The national groups, such as the Sierra Club or the Wilderness Society, are mostly located in Washington, D.C., where they direct national campaigns to educate voters on different issues and focus pressure on lawmakers. Regional or statewide groups, such as the Alliance for the Northern Rockies or the Vermont National Resources Council, pursue a more limited agenda, concentrating on issues that affect their region or state. Local groups like Green Mountain Forest Watch of Vermont or Headwaters of Oregon focus on specific local problems, such as the proposed timber sale in a local national forest or a toxic-waste dump in the area.

Work at each of these levels will present different types of opportunities. If you work in Washington, D.C., for a national group, you will spend much of your time examining federal legislation that will affect the environment, educating the public on national issues, and helping to communicate the public's opinion by dropping letters, faxes, and petitions on Capitol Hill. Work for a regional or statewide group will allow you to see how legislation affects regional ecosystems and to examine the balance between conservation groups and the industries that make up the economy of many states. Working for a local group will require you to get your hands dirty—pounding on doors, handing out petitions, or protesting to gain attention from the local news station.

You are more likely to be paid for a temporary position at one of the national groups, but the rewards of volunteer work on local problems can be quite satisfying. The environmental movement always needs young, energetic people to help with the massive job of solving our many environmental problems. You can play a crucial role and gain valuable experience for yourself.

Publications

Buzzworm: The Environmental Journal. An independent magazine reporting on national and international environmental issues, with a column listing internships, fellowships, and jobs. 1-800-825-0061

Community Jobs. Provides listings of more than 400 jobs each month. Its yearly college edition lists summer employment opportunities for students. Published by ACCESS. (617) 720-5627

Conservation Directory. Lists organizations, agencies, and personnel engaged in conservation work, natural-resources use and management at state, national, and international levels. Also lists college and universities in the U.S. and Canada that have conservation-studies programs. Published annually by the National Wildlife Federation. (202) 797-6800; 1-800-432-6564

Sea Shepherd Conservation Society. The Sea Shepherds are the environmental activists of the oceans, carrying out campaigns all around the globe. (301) 301-7325

U.S. PIRG. The PIRGs (Public Interest Research Groups) offer some terrific research and lobbying opportunities. Most PIRG employees do door-to-door canvassing, collecting signatures for ballot initiatives, or help with fund-raising for various environmental causes. Wages are at about subsistence level, but you'll generally have a neat bunch of co-workers. To find a PIRG near you, call the central office at (202) 546-9707.

Programs & Organizations

The Environmental Careers Organization. ECO offers internship opportunities for current college students and recent graduates. It publishes *The New Complete Guide to Environmental Careers,* which gives a great overview of the field and also offers some valuable information on internships. Also sponsors the Environmental Placement Services program, which matches qualified candidates with paid internships. Ask for ECO's resource list, which details dozens of job opportunities with non-profits, as well as clearinghouses for more information on jobs with environmental organizations. (617) 426-4783

Friends of the Earth. Offers internships and fellowships for college and graduate students with an interest in environmental issues. Issues include ozone depletion, environmental justice, drinking water, World Bank development projects, chemical safety, corporate accountability, indigenous peoples' rights, trade, jobs, and the environment, tax and federal budget reform, etc. (202) 544-2600

WORKING ON A KIBBUTZ IN ISRAEL

Working on an Israeli kibbutz, by all accounts, is an amazing experience. Kibbutzim are groups of people, from a few dozen to many thousands, who have pooled their assets to live communally. Most kibbutzim make a range of products, from growing fruits and vegetables to producing manufactured goods. Many kibbutzim take in volunteers. In exchange for your hard work, you receive room and board. You generally are free on the weekends, and you're liable to meet incredibly cool volunteers from all over the world.

"The best thing I can say about the experience is that it is different from anything you could do in any other country," says Margo Glantz, the national marketing director for the Kibbutz Program Center. "The idea that you can live your life without any concern for individual wealth—when it will forever be a central focus of your existence in the future—is a really amazing thing."

To get the most out of it, remember that kibbutzim have changed a great deal during this century. Many kibbutzim are largely industrial enterprises. Although your idea of working on a kibbutz may be toiling in the orange groves under the sun, you may well end up building lawn chairs in a factory.

Many volunteers complain that kibbutzniks are generally not interested in becoming friends with the volunteers, but Glantz said not to be too concerned with this. "It's definitely possible to form lasting relationships," she said. "The most important thing to remember is to show them that you care about the kibbutz as much as they do. Also, don't just assume the kibbutzniks are primitive people. Most of them have been in the army, gone to the university, and chosen this life for themselves."

Finally, remember that you don't have to be Jewish to get a lot out of the experience. One common misconception about Israelis is that they are all very religious and that non-Jews are not welcome on kibbutzim. Nothing could be further from the truth. And many kibbutzim could not survive without the volunteers.

The best way to set up a kibbutz experience from the United States is through the Kibbutz Program Center. 1-800-247-7852

WORKING ON A SCIENTIFIC OR ARCHAEOLOGICAL EXPEDITION

As a general rule, the dig jobs are easier to come by. Most scientific expeditions require you to have a science background—especially if you want to get your travel and living expenses paid for. If you've got the credentials, call your local university to see if it has an office similar to the one at the University of California at Berkeley that's listed below. A big exception to this rule is the pay-to-play programs. Earthwatch sponsors projects all over the world, while the Foundation for Field Research does mostly Caribbean programs. With both, you pay for your own travel (and with Earthwatch there is a fee for living expenses, too) for the privilege of working on everything from dolphin research to cultural anthropology projects. Most projects don't last more than a month.

Programs & Organizations

The Archaeological Institute of America. The AIA publishes an annual *Archaeological Fieldwork Opportunities Bulletin,* a must for anyone considering work on a site. It is published each year on January 1, though it's worth buying it later in the year as well, since many projects are ongoing and can last for years. 1-800-228-0810

Earthwatch. Sponsors scientific expeditions in sixty countries and twenty states in the U.S. Volunteers are required to pay their own costs, which include food, lodging, and travel to the site. The fee you pay to Earthwatch is considered a tax-deductible donation, so you may be able to funnel payment through your parents and save some money that way. Earthwatch is a membership organization, and it puts out a magazine every two months detailing some of its field opportunities. 1-800-776-0188

The Foundation for Field Research. Matches volunteers with botanists, archaeologists, primatologists, and other researchers in exotic locales. You generally have to pay your own travel expenses to get to the project. (619) 450-3460

University of California Research Expeditions Program. Its aim is to preserve endangered natural resources by building partnerships between participants, researchers, and the host country populace. Many other schools with large biology, ecology, and archaeology departments have similar clearinghouses for information on these kinds of expeditions. Call your local college or university for more information. (510) 642-6586

TRAVEL

TRAVEL ABROAD

Every year, tens of thousands of college students get their bachelor's degrees and embark on the victory tour, treading the well-worn paths through the European capitals on their parents' money. Not a bad way to spend a summer, and if you can get your parents to fund a trip like this during your time off, more power to you. For most of you, though, this kind of trip won't be an option. Europe may seem so enticing that you want to go, anyway. You're young, you're healthy. Who says you can't do Europe on ten dollars a day? Sean Fitzpatrick, former publishing director of the *Let's Go* travel books, remembered this feeling well. "When I was a researcher for *Let's Go* in Ireland, I subsisted on Pop-Tarts and slept in abandoned cars for two months," he said.

Fitzpatrick ultimately decided that he preferred a less extreme mode of traveling. "It's easy to push yourself past your limits. Particularly in Europe, people will do things—like subsisting on Pop-Tarts—that they wouldn't normally consider. Living low-to-the-ground like that is a really good way to just waste away. People taking an extended amount of time off should really think seriously about Third World destinations, where your dollar goes further," he said. Fitzpatrick knows from experience, having taken a semester off from Harvard to travel through South America. "There, people travel according to currency fluctuations. When the exchange rate rose in Brazil, everyone went to Paraguay. People didn't feel that there was that much to do there, but it was all part of spending as much time on the road as humanly possible," he added. If you're absolutely wedded to the idea of at least being close to Europe, consider the former Eastern-bloc nations, Turkey, or Morocco.

Once you get there, don't think that the guidelines for healthy living that you followed in the States don't apply anymore. "When people backpack abroad, it may be the first time they haven't had mom or the dorm there to take care of them," Fitzpatrick said. "Some people quickly realize how many habits aren't really all that deeply ingrained. Do I really have to change my underwear or brush my teeth or eat three meals a day? But the most successful travelers are the ones who can recall which country the pyramids were in, after they've been to twenty countries. Inevitably, those people are the ones who have bathed and groomed and maintained some sense of civility." Another caveat: Drugs will be remarkably easy to get in many places that you visit. They can also land you in rat-infested jails for a very long time.

Gear-wise, you don't want to be penny wise and pound foolish. A good guidebook will pay for itself within days. Let's Go and Lonely Planet Guides are the best ones to get; bringing both is not a bad idea. You may not want to look like a travel-book-toting tourist, but you will attract other travelers who haven't brought their own guides. You may think you want to avoid other travelers and soak up only the local culture and that's fine. Chances are, however, you'll want to hang out with some like-minded people sooner or later. The books will help get you to places where you'll find others like you, since they're reading the same books. Don't skimp on your backpack, either. "You spend more time with your pack than anything else," Fitzpatrick reminded. "I spent $150 on mine, which was a great bargain. But every time it started biting my ribs I wondered why I didn't spend even more."

Programs & Organizations

EuropeBOUND. Three-part video series on how to plan a cheap trip to Europe, produced by CIEE.

U.S. State Department. Country reports may be obtained by calling (202) 647-5225. These reports are updated often, with information about safety and health issues in your country of choice.

TRAVEL IN THE U.S.

Publications

Rolling Nowhere, by Ted Conover. Penguin, 1985. The book Ted wrote about his experiences riding freight trains with hoboes.

Programs & Organizations

National Outdoor Leadership School. NOLS offers wilderness education expeditions in the U.S. and abroad. The trips emphasize the acquisition of basic outdoor skills and teach students how to make a minimum impact on the environment. Programs range in length from two weeks to a semester. Financial aid is available. (307) 332-6973

Outward Bound. Outward Bound runs challenging outdoor education programs which range in length from three weeks to a semester. (914) 424-4000

Appalachian Mountain Club. This is the organization that promotes and maintains the Appalachian Trail. It can suggest the best books to read before heading out on a hike. (304) 535-6331

TRAVELING ON A BICYCLE

Few experiences can compare to taking a long-distance bicycle trip. Bicycle touring is the ultimate freedom, a mode of travel that allows you to stop at all the small towns, roadside vegetable stands, and dairy farms that the trains, buses, and planes pass by as they rush from city to city. You may set out on a bike expedition of your own choosing, sign up with a company that will provide a tour of two to twelve weeks, or join a cause-related fund-raising bike tour.

"The back roads of America offer great opportunities for cyclists—fantastic scenery, friendly people, and wonderful bicycling," said Gary MacFadden, executive director of the Adventure Cycling Association. The Adventure Cycling Association has a route network of over 20,000 miles. "Maps include the TransAmerica Bicycle Trail, which follows the historic growth of the nation; the Southern Tier, which meanders through the Old South; and the Northern Tier, which explores the Northern states and parts of Canada," MacFadden said.

To set out on your own bike expedition, alone or with friends, requires some planning but is fairly simple. The first and most important decision is choosing your route. The western coast of the United States is popular, as is riding across the country from San Francisco to Washington, D.C. Look for a region where you can utilize the secondary highways, camping grounds and hostels, and see beautiful scenery along the way.

For some, it is easier to sign up with an organized tour, where the operator provides the bicycles, equipment, route, and food—all you do is pay. These tours can range from rustic to plush, from campfire cooking to sliced honeydew melons awaiting you at each resting point. If you are unable to organize your own trip or do not feel safe riding alone, these tours can be an enjoyable alternative.

Another interesting option is joining one of the rising number of cause-related bike tours. One such tour, Bike-Aid, sends young people rolling across the country, doing educational workshops about AIDS in the small towns they pass through.

Whatever your choice, the pure simplicity of rolling down the road with only the necessary possessions strapped to your bike is not to be missed.

When planning your own bike trip, your first stop should be a bike shop. The bike-shop staff is liable to be very knowledgeable on what kinds of gear to take, where to go, and who else to talk to for more information. Many large camping-supply stores have a book section, so check there as well as in regular bookstores for books on good biking trips. Travel bookstores may be helpful as well.

Publications

Bicycling Magazine's Bike Touring in the 90's, by Bicycling Magazine Editors. Rodale Press, 1993. Covers the United States and Europe, and contains a great guide to planned tours.

Bicycle Magazine's Long Distance Cycling, by Bicycling Magazine Editors. Rodale Press, 1993. Covers technique, training, and general bike maintenance.

The Essential Touring Cyclist, by Richard A. Lovett. McGraw-Hill, 1994. A truly comprehensive book which includes a great section on buying a bicycle.

Bike Abroad: 439 Organized Trips with 70 Companies in 49 Countries, by Gerri Alpert. New Voyager Trip Finders, 1995.

Programs & Organizations

Adventure Cycling Association. An excellent information source for cyclists, this organization can help you plan your bike trip. They also publish detailed bike maps for the United States which allow you to travel cross-country without ever seeing an interstate highway. The maps include information on bicycling conditions, local history, and services that cyclists need (such as location of bike shops, campgrounds and motels, and grocery stores). (406) 721-1776

Bicycle Federation of America. This is a great place to start. The helpful staff can steer you in the right direction according to your individual needs. (202) 332-6986

Bike-Aid. A program sponsored by the Overseas Development Network (ODN), which sends young people on cross-country bike trips to do AIDS education and other workshops. (415) 431-4480

International Bicycle Fund. Publishes books on bicycle travel in Africa and throughout the world. (206) 628-9314

STUDY

POST-GRADUATE ACADEMIC YEARS IN THE U.S.

If you're interested in brushing up on your academic or sports skills, you may want to consider a post-graduate or "13th year" option at a boarding school. Motivations for a "PG" year vary. Some students hope to cap off a successful high school career at a mediocre school with one year of outstanding grades and extracurriculars at a well-known boarding school before applying to college. Other students simply feel unprepared to do college-level work and need an extra year to ready themselves. The programs tend to be expensive, but they can help you get into a better college. Ask your high school guidance counselor for more information.

ACADEMIC PROGRAMS ABROAD/LEARNING A FOREIGN LANGUAGE ABROAD

Are you interested in learning Kiswahili on an island off the coast of Kenya? Would you enjoy studying Italian sculpture in Florence? Does living with a Mexican family while attending a local high school in Mexico City entice you? Studying abroad is not limited to juniors in college anymore, nor is it limited to people with lots of cash. Whether you have a month or a year, you can have an amazing learning experience in nearly every corner of the globe.

If your goal is to learn a foreign language, the best place to learn it is where it is spoken. Many countries have language schools for foreigners in their capitals. In most countries outside of Europe, enrolling in these language schools is inexpensive and easy. The difficult part may be locating the schools before leaving the States. We have included a list of resources that may help you pick out a language school before you leave. Of particular use is Transitions Abroad's *Alternative Travel Directory,* which provides a country-by-country listing of local language institutes. You should also look at the Lonely Planet travel guides for the countries where you would be interested in studying. These guides list local language schools that have been recommended by their readers. Many language schools offer opportunities to live inexpensively with local families while you are studying. Although moving in with perfect strangers does have its drawbacks, it is a great way to have a twenty-four-hour language experience. Living with a local family can also give an insider's perspective into the country's culture.

If you want to study abroad for a semester, your high school or college should have information available about various programs. The prices, quality, and style of programs vary widely, so be sure to talk to past program participants. If you find the information and materials at your school insufficient, you may want to call a large university near you that has a study-abroad office or international-affairs deparatment with more resources. In addition, the following organizations and books should be a good starting point.

Publications

Study Abroad 1995: A Guide to Semester & Year Abroad Academic Programs. Peterson's Guides, 1994.

Programs & Organizations

American Field Studies Intercultural programs. AFS arranges exchanges for high school students in dozens of countries. Students live with a family and take classes at the local high school. Financial aid is available. 1-800-AFS-INFO

American International Youth Student Exchange Program. AIYSEP sends students to Europe, Australia, New Zealand, and the former Soviet Union for a semester or a year on a home-stay exchange program. Students attend classes at local public high schools. Financial aid is available. (415) 499-7669

The Rotary Club. Rotary is an international service organization whose members are usually businesspeople. It has chapters in nearly every major city in the world. Local branches sponsor exchanges for students who have not yet attended college. Rotary provides students with airfare, room, board, and a small stipend. You can contact your local Rotary Club for information, or call the national headquarters at (708) 866-3000.

Open Door Student Exchange. ODSE sponsors study programs in Europe and Australia. Financial aid is available. (516) 745-6232

Semester at Sea. Students spend six weeks on land studying oceanography and nautical science and then spend six weeks sailing on one of the program's two boats. Financial aid is available. Call the Sea Education Association for more information. (508) 540-3954

Young Judaea Year Course in Israel. High school graduates spend nine months studying, traveling, and volunteering in Israel. (212) 303-4594

HELP ON THE WAY

Acknowledgments

Many people took time off from their busy lives to help us complete this book. To begin with, we would like to give a special thanks to Joel Zemans. When we came to him in the fall of 1993, our enthusiasm for this book was our only collateral. Joel gave us a loan anyway, and his generosity enabled us to travel around the country to conduct our interviews.

Early on, Elisa Tamarkin and Kim Townsend convinced us that a book proposal was not the same thing as a five-paragraph essay. Ben Lieber and Susan Little dispensed excellent advice on what a book like this should include. Mary Berger and Norman Newell gave us valuable advice on self-publishing. We must also thank Michael Lee Cohen, Ted Conover, and Chris Ogden, who convinced us that we needed an agent and helped us find one.

We owe appreciation to Mike DeBeer, whose computer expertise enabled us to flood the Internet with our request for stories from people who had taken time off. When we hit the road to start tracking people down in person, a number of people put us up or put up with us. Thanks to David Korduner and Joan Krimston, Josh Krimston and Celine Faccini, Fran and Monte Krimston, the Quezadas and the Steeles, and Christina Hall and Peter Wald. We are also grateful to the people at Jenner & Block, especially Sharon Webb and Joan Gill, who helped us in innumerable ways while we were completing the manuscript. Carrie Bader, Mandy Field, Erin Kaufman, Jennifer Mattson, Sarah Nasonchuk, and Ilya Somin all noticed mistakes in the manuscript that had eluded us. When our Resources section needed a third set of eyes, Barbara Messing stepped in and brought it to a whole new level.

Colin: Much appreciation goes to Larry Gray, who encouraged me to take risks; to Barry Childress, who helped me learn to listen to other people's stories; and to Marie Stone and Pat Nagle, who always taught their students that anything is possible. I also wish to thank Ann Jones, Stanley Rabinowitz, Ilan Stavans, and Helen von Schmidt for encouraging my writing. Additional thanks go to my male, and female, roommates at Amherst. I would like to thank Warren, Delia, Jim and Lori McClurg; Lynn Hall; the Cotsirilos and Wheeler clans; as well as my friends at Morgan Stanley, all of whom have shown a sincere interest in taking time off, literally.

Ron: A special tip of the cap to Terry Allen, who opened the pages of *Amherst* magazine to me. I'm also grateful to Ann Jones, who encouraged me to take my work to an even wider audience, and to Stan Moulton and Debra Scherban, who gave me some terrific opportunities at the *Daily Hampshire Gazette*. In a very short time, Roz Berlin and my colleagues at *Fortune* have taught me some valuable lessons about accuracy, and I hope it shows in these pages. Tom Harrison and Marian Jones at *Lawyers Weekly USA* put up with my odd scheduling requests, and Aaron Grossman and Susan Cardoza quietly endured my zealous use of the phone in our stable there. Thanks also to my roommates: Dan Chiasson, Kyle Johnson, Chris Perry, Steve Stutman, Frank Tan, and Bibie Wu, who offered unfailing encouragement and put up with my strange hours. Finally, I'd like to thank my Uncle Frank and Aunt MaryLiz for things too numerous to list here.

Neither of us would be where we are today without our teachers at the Francis W. Parker School in Chicago. During our fourteen years there, they promoted a vision of an education which extended beyond the four walls of the classroom. We hope the spirit behind Parker's progressive education is reflected in the stories we have collected for this book. In particular, we owe appreciation to Harriett Cholden, John Cotton, Barnaby Dinges, Joel Dure, Bill Duffy, Diane Fitzgerald, Dan Frank, Dren Geer, Karen Harrison, Andy Kaplan, Connie Kelly, Bernard Markwell, Pat McHale, Bob Merrick, Bonnie Seebold, Marie Stone, and Roger Wallenstein.

When we first called Anne Edelstein, she had recently become a mother for the first time. We asked her to adopt us, she agreed, and having her as our agent has been invaluable. Her assistants, Hilary Howard and Corinna Snyder, have been extremely helpful. When Anne called to tell us that Elisabeth Kallick Dyssegaard wanted to see us in her office at Farrar, Straus and Giroux, we thought at first there must have been a mistake. We were greeted by a gentle and precise editor—the antithesis of what we had expected to find in the New York City publishing milieu. Her assistants, Joan Mathieu and Denise Oswald, gave us helpful feedback.

We have many friends in common whose support and encouragement we would like to recognize. Kate Alberg, Josh

Anderson, Christine Bader, Matt Brown, the Buchanan family, Steve Burwell, Megan Carr, Katerina Christopoulos, Al Decker, Jim Feldman, Rachel Gordon, Kim Kamin, Eric Klinenberg, Seoni Llanes, Melanie Nutter, Mike Ogden, Audrey Patt, Jeff Posternak, Meghan Searl, Matt Siegel, Owen Stearns, Deborah Wexler, and Nick Zerbib have all given us immeasurable support throughout this project.

The best part of writing this book was meeting the people we profiled. They invited two perfect strangers into their lives and trusted us to do justice to their stories. There would, quite literally, be no book without them.

Finally, we would like to thank our families, especially our parents, Charlene Lieber, Fred Lieber, Joan Hall, and George Cotsirilos, who have always loved, supported, and believed in their sons. As for our younger siblings, Justin Hall, David Lieber, and Stephanie Lieber, we simply hope that they will take the advice in these pages to heart.